ATLANTA
FALCONS

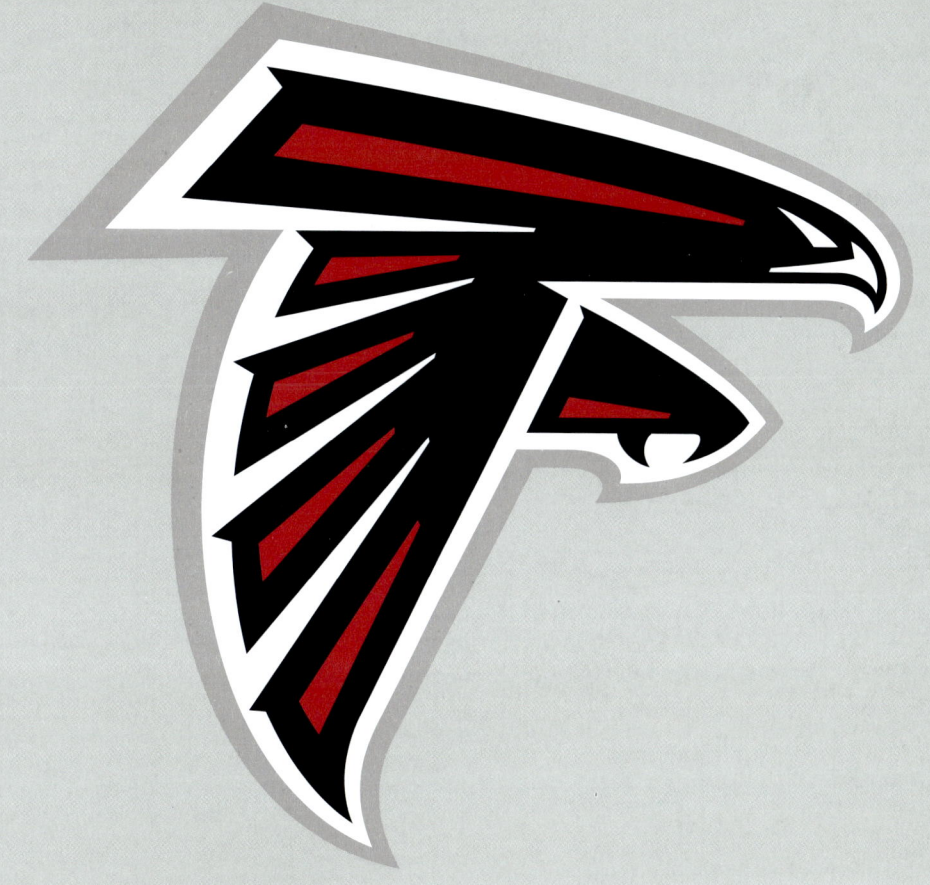

HIGH FLYING FALCONS—The First Season of a New Era
Senior Editor: John P. Holms
Graphic Designer: Chad Owen
Writer: George Henry
Photographer (Interior and Cover): Jimmy Cribb
Copy Chief: Terri Fredrickson
Copy and Production Editor: Victoria Forlini
Editorial Operations Manager: Karen Schirm
Managers, Book Production: Pam Kvitne, Marjorie J. Schenkelberg, Rick von Holdt
Contributing Copy Editors: Randy Brubaker, Tina White, Lori Blachford
Contributing Proofreader: Margaret Smith
Electronic Production Coordinator: Paula Forest
Editorial and Design Assistants: Renee E. McAtee, Karen McFadden

Meredith® Books
Editor in Chief: Linda Raglan Cunningham
Design Director: Matt Strelecki
Executive Editor: Benjamin W. Allen

Publisher: James D. Blume
Executive Director, Marketing: Jeffrey Myers
Executive Director, New Business Development: Todd M. Davis
Executive Director, Sales: Ken Zagor
Director, Operations: George A. Susral
Director, Production: Douglas M. Johnston
Business Director: Jim Leonard

Vice President and General Manager: Douglas J. Guendel

Meredith Publishing Group
President, Publishing Group: Stephen M. Lacy
Vice President-Publishing Director: Bob Mate

Meredith Corporation
Chairman and Chief Executive Officer: William T. Kerr

Chairman of the Executive Committee: E. T. Meredith III

For other Meredith books check wherever quality books are sold.
Or visit us at: meredithbooks.com

© Copyright 2003 by Meredith Corporation. First Edition.
All rights reserved. Printed in the United States of America.
Library of Congress Control Number: 2003104428
ISBN: 0-696-21889-5

Distributed by Meredith Corporation

THE FIRST SEASON OF A NEW ERA

Falcons chairman, president and CEO Arthur Blank and executive vice president of marketing Dick Sullivan reveal the Falcons new team logo during a press conference at the team's Flowery Branch headquarters in March 2003. Also in the offing are redesigned uniforms. The new look is just one example of how the Falcons are focusing on the future and intent on becoming a serious contender in the NFL.

Win games. Make game days more exciting. Give something back to the state of Georgia. These are the promises of a three-point plan Arthur Blank presented to the fans when he purchased the team in 2002. If that's not enough Blank has also promised he won't rest until the Falcons own a Super Bowl trophy. The excitement generated on and off the field in 2002 indicates that he's already delivering. The Falcons are flying high and the future for football is bright in Atlanta.

HIGH FLYING FALCONS—*The First Season of a New Era* is the story of a magical season. And, most importantly, it's a story about the people—the players, the management, and the fans who, together, are ushering in a new era.

The story of the 2002 Falcons includes a number of turning points that are shaping a new direction:
- Arthur Blank purchases the team
- Michael Vick assumes the role of starting quarterback
- The phenomenal midseason 8-game unbeaten streak that shakes up the NFL
- The exciting upset of Green Bay in the playoffs at Lambeau Field that turns fans into believers.

It's a story of what happens when new ideas and new talent infuse an organization with a will to win:
- Falcons management is teaming Michael Vick with talented and committed players. A lot of them, including Keith Brooking, Patrick Kerney, Bob Whitfield, Warrick Dunn, and T.J. Duckett are already in Falcons uniforms. Peerless Price and others are on the way.

It's a story about community building and commitment to a great city and state:
- Individual players are giving back with their foundations and their time
- Blank encourages and expects all Falcons associates to engage themselves in community service.

Head coach Dan Reeves speaks for himself, the team, and the organization when he says, "It's made my life so much better, my job so much more fun, that it's hard to put into words."

That's the purpose of this book—to tell the story of the exciting 2002 season and take a glimpse into the future. What follows are words and pictures describing what the Falcons were, where they are now, and what they will become. The news is out. It's a great time to be a Falcons fan.

George Henry
Flowery Branch, Georgia—April 2003

HIGH FLYING FALCONS

THE FIRST SEASON OF A NEW ERA

TABLE OF CONTENTS

INTRODUCTION 4.21.01 Picking Vick **8**
    PROFILE: **TEN GREATEST PLAYERS IN FALCONS HISTORY** **14**
    PROFILE: **A BLANK SLATE—LIFE BEFORE ARTHUR** **19**

CHAPTER ONE 2.02.02 Falcons Receive a Blank Check **22**
    PROFILE: **ARTHUR BLANK** **32**

CHAPTER TWO 2.25.02 Michael's the Man **34**
    PROFILE: **RETOOLING THE PLAYBOOK** **36**
    PROFILE: **DAN REEVES** **46**

CHAPTER THREE Training Camp **50**
    PROFILE: **DICK SULLIVAN** **54**
    PROFILE: **PATRICK KERNEY** **58**

CHAPTER FOUR The Preseason **62**

CHAPTER FIVE Been There, Done That—Games 1-4 .... **74**
    PROFILE: **BOB WHITFIELD** **78**

CHAPTER SIX Giant Killers—Games 5-8 .... **86**
    PROFILE: **DOUG JOHNSON** **88**

CHAPTER SEVEN Cloud of Dust—Games 9-10 .... **98**
    PROFILE: **WARRICK DUNN** **102**

CHAPTER EIGHT Pass the Magic—Games 11-12 .... **108**
    PROFILE: **KEITH BROOKING** **112**
    PROFILE: **THE DEFENSE** **119**
    PROFILE: **THE RUN** **120**

CHAPTER NINE Reality Check—Games 13-16 .... **122**
    PROFILE: **THE FANS** **126**

CHAPTER TEN Making Believers—The Playoffs **136**
    PROFILE: **T.J. DUCKETT** **140**
    PROFILE: **ON THE ROAD AGAIN—TRAVELING WITH THE TEAM** **146**

CHAPTER ELEVEN The Start of a New Era—Crafting a Winner **150**
    PROFILE: **THE EXTRA MILE** **156**

INTRODUCTION

4.21.2001 PICKING VICK

They had celebrated just eight winning years in Atlanta's 36 seasons in the NFL, but the faithful sensed great changes on the horizon. Fans flocked by the thousands to witness the moment when the Falcons would draft Michael Vick, a quarterback whose talent and potential were unquestioned. Was Atlanta on the verge of something big?

The potential of Falcons quarterback Michael Vick is evident to players throughout the NFL, including former teammate Chris Chandler. "It's going to be fun down the road to see him turn into the player everyone thinks he can be," Chandler says.

INTRODUCTION 9

*F*lowery Branch appears no different from other sleepy residential communities on the northern end of Atlanta's suburban sprawl. Schools, shopping centers, and gated neighborhoods rise from the soil of abandoned cow pastures. Sounds of gravel are a memory on winding country roads, now repaved and rerouted to meet increased demand.

Change is inevitable, but, still, every year in mid-April, azaleas, dogwoods, and redbuds wake up to ask questions that daffodils, camellias, and cherry trees posed a month earlier. "Is it spring yet?"

Easy answer. Spring certainly dominates the Georgia landscape on April 21, 2001, and no place looks as freshly affected as the eight-month-old home of the Atlanta Falcons.

AFTER THE SEASONS WE'VE BEEN THROUGH, IT'S IMPORTANT TO GET THE CITY EXCITED ABOUT THIS TEAM AGAIN. —DAN REEVES ON THE SIGNING OF MICHAEL VICK

SO, WHAT'S NEW?

On this warm April day, waves of people pull their vehicles off to the side of Falcon Parkway. No sidewalks line this short stretch of Georgia Highway 13. No signs point to a planned event. True, the team has invited season-ticket holders to attend a draft-day party at an indoor practice field, but they expect fewer than 1,200 to attend.

Instead, Highway 13 is a parking lot and the Falcons complex is swarming with football fans. Approximately 10,000

Calm, poised, and focused in the midst of a media storm, Michael Vick displays his new team's jersey signifying that he's the No. 1 pick. Football is a team effort; no single player can carry a team. But this phenomenal young athlete from Virginia Tech could be the catalyst the Falcons need to forge a winner. He's smart, savvy, and eager to make the transition from college star to the NFL.

No draft dodgers in Flowery Branch on this April day. The fans get ready to go wild as they await the televised appearance of Michael "No. 1" Vick, live from New York.

eager onlookers have brought Flowery Branch its first traffic jam.

The team hadn't anticipated this kind of turnout, but the fans don't care. They're determined to be together on the day the Atlanta Falcons draft Virginia Tech's phenomenal young quarterback, Michael Vick.

WANTED: IMPACT PLAYER

In the NFL, teams can generate excitement and bring fans back to the stadium with a few victories. A rookie quarterback such as Vick is worth even more. No fan can miss the buzz surrounding this guy. He runs the 40-yard dash in a dazzling 4.3 seconds and has a cannon for a left arm. This

INTRODUCTION 11

20-year-old has enough smarts, poise, swagger, and humility to become a real leader.

Coach Dan Reeves and the front office staff know they must act boldly. San Diego, which owns the No. 1 pick, is impressed with Vick, but the Chargers are still reeling from their 1998 decision to select quarterback Ryan Leaf in the second overall spot. It was a great surprise—especially for the Chargers! Leaf turned out to be one of the biggest busts in the history of the draft.

So the day before the 2001 draft, the Falcons traded three picks—a first-rounder (No. 5 overall), a third-rounder, and a second-rounder in 2002—along with receiver Tim Dwight to San Diego for the rights to select Vick.

Now the fans are congregating at the Falcons complex on this fine April day because maybe, just maybe, they smell a winner. Anyone could have watched the draft pick at home on television, but Vick's talent is so alluring that crowds of fans have gathered to watch the big screen as this soft-spoken native of Newport News, Va. shakes the hand of NFL Commissioner Paul Tagliabue. Cheers fill the practice facility as the commissioner places a Falcons cap on Vick's head.

Dan Reeves is clearly excited as well. "I was not expecting to ride down the freeway and have people giving me this," Reeves grins, giving the assembled crowd a big thumbs up. "After the seasons we've been through, it's important to get the city excited about this team again."

Maybe Vick can feel it too. Though he's standing at a podium 800 miles away in New York City, this talented youngster is very much present. Reporters ask if fans can expect him to make an immediate impact on the team.

Words like "savior" make Vick uncomfortable. Already aware that he'll spend his rookie season playing behind Atlanta starter Chris Chandler, Vick wisely gives an indirect answer.

"One thing they have to understand is that I am not going to make things happen in one game," Vick says. "It's going to take some time."

Turns out he's not only a player, he's a prophet.

WELCOME TO THE NFL—VICK'S FIRST SEASON

The 2001 season starts with a plan that proves tough to execute. Chandler, the veteran, is Reeves' No.1 quarterback, but the coach wants to carve out playing time for his prize rookie too. When Chandler struggles to keep his rhythm,

Continued on page 18

The Georgia Dome has seen its share of empty seats, but hard-core fans have stuck by the team through thick and thin. With the signing of Michael Vick and a spate of aggressive off-season moves, maybe the fans will really have something to cheer about in the coming years.

12 ATLANTA FALCONS

Morten Andersen kicked Atlanta into the Super Bowl in January 1999, but soon it was business as usual. Fans started assuming the light at the end of the tunnel was an approaching freight train. What went wrong?

NO. 7 ... CATALYST FOR CHANGE?

Michael Vick was immediately a cause for celebration, and why not? This kid was for real. The Atlanta faithful have followed the Falcons, despite the fact that the team, which first took the field in 1966, had never managed consecutive winning seasons.

Not long after Morten Andersen kicked the game-winning overtime field goal in the 1998 NFC championship thriller at Minnesota, the Falcons began to fall back into old patterns.

In the days before their first and only trip to the Super Bowl ended in a decisive loss to Denver, the Falcons worked furiously at undermining their success. A series of errors in judgment, gaffs, untimely personal admissions, prideful guarantees of victory, and unfortunate encounters with Miami law enforcement sent the team into a public freefall that overshadowed a glorious year.

The Falcons were just coming off the second divisional title in team history and a 16-win season that included an NFL-record 410 carries by running back Jamal Anderson.

But after Denver won the Super Bowl 34-19, the Falcons cut leading receiver Tony Martin and leading tackler Cornelius Bennett. Reeves, overcome with confidence early in the 1999 draft, traded Atlanta's first-round pick in 2000 to Baltimore so the Falcons could select tight end Reggie Kelly in the second round.

Just two weeks into the fall of 1999, a torn knee ligament ended Anderson's season. A 0-4 start sent Atlanta spiraling to a 5-11 finish. Then Reeves, whose agent and close friend Robert Fraley died in the same October plane crash that killed golfer Payne Stewart, had to watch the following April as the Ravens chose Tennessee running back Jamal Lewis with the No. 5 overall pick they acquired from Atlanta.

By the end of 2000, the Super Bowl journey felt a decade old. Anderson returned, but a paper-thin offensive line gave him no room to run. The Falcons went 4-12.

Entering 2001, the South's oldest NFL franchise was an all-time 113 games under .500. How disproportionate were these numbers? Consider that the 1972 Miami Dolphins were the last team with a perfect record and that Atlanta could have gone unbeaten over the next seven regular seasons and still would have been one game under the break-even mark.

"Same old Falcons," went the chorus. Changing the tune became the top priority for everyone involved with the team. Where do you start? Go after the best available players. Find the talent and get them in Falcons uniforms. Build an organization to support them. Find a catalyst to light the fire.

The stage is set at the Georgia Dome for a savior. Would he come from Virginia Tech? On draft day 2001, 10,000 fans think it's a possibility.

INTRODUCTION

TEN GREATEST PLAYERS IN FALCONS HISTORY

#1 TOMMY NOBIS / Linebacker

YEARS: 1966-76

ACQUIRED: Drafted No. 1 overall out of Texas.

DEPARTED: Retired when his knees finally gave out.

ACCOMPLISHMENTS: Five Pro Bowls; named to NFL's All-Decade team for the 1960s.

SUMMARY: No opposing player wanted to run near the middle of the Atlanta defense in Nobis' rookie year. According to numbers kept by the Falcons, Nobis had 296 tackles, including 173 solo stops, in '66. His hits were so devastating that Dallas running back Don Perkins told editors of *Total Football* that Nobis "was the toughest middle linebacker I ever played against."

TODAY: The first draft pick in the history of the franchise now works as the Falcons vice president of corporate development. He also serves on the board of the Tommy Nobis Center, a 25-year-old training complex in Marietta that helps disabled youth and adults find jobs.

#2 STEVE BARTKOWSKI — Quarterback

YEARS: 1975-85
ACQUIRED: Drafted No. 1 overall out of California.
DEPARTED: Placed on waivers Nov. 26, 1985. Signed for the final month with Washington and played six games in '86 for the Los Angeles Rams before retiring.
ACCOMPLISHMENTS: Two Pro Bowls; Falcons career passing leader in completions (1,870), attempts (3,329), yards (23,468), and touchdowns (154).
SUMMARY: The golden boy with movie-star looks and one of the best arms of his era, Bartkowski rose to prominence on cold, rainy Christmas Eve in 1978 with two fourth-quarter TD passes in the Falcons first playoff game, a 14-13 victory over Philadelphia.
TODAY: A member of the Falcons board of directors since March 2002, and an avid golfer and outdoorsman, he works with DPR Construction in Atlanta.

#3 CLAUDE HUMPHREY — Defensive end

YEARS: 1968-74, '76-78
ACQUIRED: Drafted No. 3 overall out of Tennessee State.
DEPARTED: Retired after four games in 1978, was traded in '79 to Philadelphia, and played three years with the Eagles before retiring again.
ACCOMPLISHMENTS: Six Pro Bowls. Racked up 94.5 career sacks, despite missing 1975 with knee surgery.
SUMMARY: Though Carl Eller, L.C. Greenwood, Harvey Martin, and Jack Youngblood were the four ends named to the NFL's All-Decade team for the 1970s, Humphrey was as good as any of them. He twice had a five-sack game for Atlanta and ended five seasons with 10 or more sacks.
TODAY: Lives on a farm in Tennessee.

#4 MICHAEL VICK — Quarterback

YEARS: 2001-
ACQUIRED: Drafted No. 1 overall out of Virginia Tech.
ACCOMPLISHMENTS: One Pro Bowl; set single-game NFL rushing record by a quarterback with 173 yards at Minnesota in 2002; only quarterback to rush for at least 90 yards in two consecutive games; has run for more yards in his first two seasons (1,066) than any QB in history.
SUMMARY: If he stays healthy, Vick will become one of the all-time great players at his position. The Falcons have only begun to tap into his ability as a passer.
TODAY: Lives in Duluth, Ga., and Newport News, Va.

INTRODUCTION 15

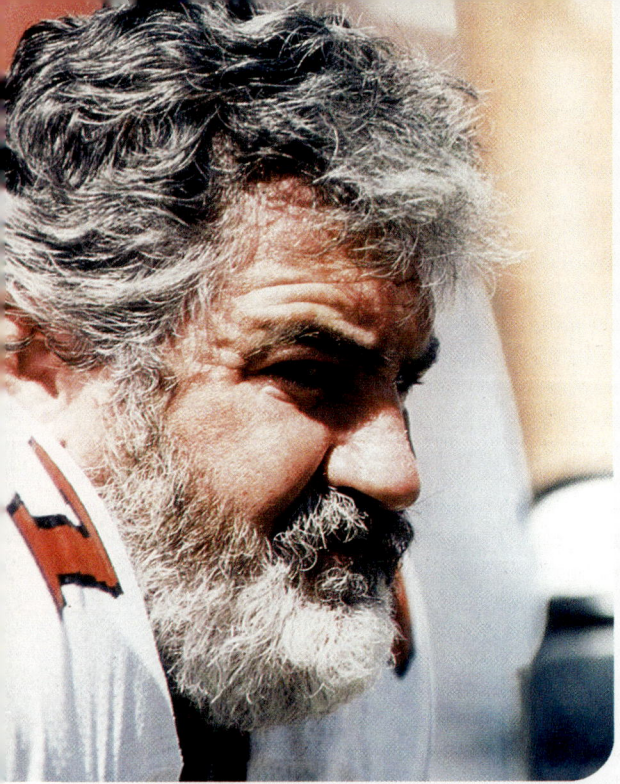

#6 GERALD RIGGS — Running back

YEARS: 1982-88
ACQUIRED: Drafted No. 9 overall out of Arizona State.
DEPARTED: Traded during the 1989 NFL draft to Washington, where he scored two TDs in the Redskins' Super Bowl victory over Buffalo two seasons later.
ACCOMPLISHMENTS: Three Pro Bowls; Atlanta's career rushing leader in yards (6,631), attempts (1,587), most 100-yard games (25), most TDs (48).
SUMMARY: Riggs was one of the few reasons to watch the Falcons in his heyday from '84-87, a four-year stretch that ended with an 18-44-1 record. A knee injury forced him to miss seven games in '88, and the Falcons, content to give his job to John Settle, obliged Riggs' request for a trade. In Riggs' last five years with Atlanta, only Hall of Fame running back Eric Dickerson, who finished his career in Atlanta, gained more yards than Riggs' 5,895.
TODAY: Lives in Chattanooga, Tenn.

#5 JEFF VAN NOTE — Center

YEARS: 1969-86.
ACQUIRED: Drafted in the 11th round out of Kentucky.
DEPARTED: Retired after playing his entire career in Atlanta.
ACCOMPLISHMENTS: Six Pro Bowls; played more seasons (18) and consecutive games (155) than any other Falcon.
SUMMARY: William Andrews and Gerald Riggs were two of the game's better running backs 1979-86, and Van Note was a big reason why.
TODAY: Worked past six years as color commentator with team's radio network.

#7 WILLIAM ANDREWS — Running back

YEARS: 1979-83, '86
ACQUIRED: Drafted in third round out of Auburn.
DEPARTED: Major knee injury that sidelined him for 1984-85 finally forced Andrews to retire after a one-year comeback.
ACCOMPLISHMENTS: Four Pro Bowls; Atlanta career leader in yards per carry (4.6), second all-time in rushing yards (5,986) and attempts (1,315), and third in TDs (30).
SUMMARY: Andrews joined Walter Payton, Wilbur Montgomery, and O.J. Simpson as the only running backs to have at least 2,000 total yards in their first year. In '79-83, Andrews led the NFL with 8,382 total yards.
TODAY: Lives in Suwanee, Ga.

#8 JESSIE TUGGLE / Linebacker

YEARS: 1987-2000
ACQUIRED: Undrafted free agent from Valdosta State.
DEPARTED: Retired on August 28, 2001.
ACCOMPLISHMENTS: Five Pro Bowls; Falcons career leader in tackles (2,065) and third in seasons played (14), starts (189) and games (209); named NFC defensive player of the month in December 1991.
SUMMARY: Nicknamed "The Hammer," Tuggle had 12 straight 100-tackle seasons and set an NFL record by scoring five touchdowns on fumble returns.
TODAY: Lives in Alpharetta, Ga.

#9 DEION SANDERS / Cornerback, punt-kickoff returner

YEARS: 1989-93
ACQUIRED: Drafted No. 5 overall out of Florida State.
DEPARTED: Signed free-agent contract with San Francisco and earned two straight Super Bowl rings, one with 49ers and another with Dallas.
ACCOMPLISHMENTS: Three Pro Bowls with Atlanta; Falcons career leader in total return yards (4,177) and in total TD returns (8) on kickoffs, punts, and interceptions; named NFC defensive player of the month in November 1992.
SUMMARY: "Prime Time" lived up to the nickname, becoming a two-sport star in baseball stints with the Atlanta Braves, New York Yankees, San Francisco Giants, and Cincinnati Reds. He's the only person to play in a World Series and a Super Bowl. No one else has hit a major-league home run and scored an NFL touchdown in the same week.
TODAY: Lives in Dallas and works as an NFL analyst for CBS Sports.

#10 MIKE KENN / Left tackle

YEARS: 1978-94
ACQUIRED: Drafted No. 13 overall out of Michigan.
DEPARTED: Ailing back forced him to announce retirement in '94.
ACCOMPLISHMENTS: Five Pro Bowls; Falcons career leader in games played (251) and second in number of seasons (17).
SUMMARY: Only George Blanda, Jim Marshall, Jan Stenerud, Earl Morrall, and Jackie Slater played in more games. Kenn played in the Falcons first stretch of success. Claude Humphrey was the only other Atlanta player to make five straight Pro Bowls.
TODAY: Lives in Atlanta and serves as chairman of the Fulton County Commission.

Continued from page 12

Vick's playing time suffers. The Falcons enter December with a 6-4 record, but a nonexistent pass defense costs them five of the last six games. By the time Chandler is knocked out of a 35-6 loss to St. Louis in Week 12, Vick has played only twice in the last six games.

The Rams fluster Vick, whom they sack twice and force into five hurried throws. He completes only seven of 18 passes in a 35-6 loss and sits out the next three weeks.

Returning in a Week 16 loss at Miami after Chandler injures an elbow, Vick loses a fumble and throws an interception. But somewhere in the fourth quarter, Vick discovers the savvy for spectacular plays he exhibited at Virginia Tech. Brushing aside Atlanta's gloomy, predictable past, Vick gives a performance that radiates hope for 2002. The Dolphins hold on for a 21-14 win that ends Atlanta's playoff hopes, but it's a moral victory.

"He gave us a chance to win," receiver Shawn Jefferson says after catching a 48-yard bullet Vick throws off-balance as he scrambles to his left. "He took control in the huddle. That's something you don't always see in a rookie."

THE FUTURE IS ALMOST NOW

The Falcons 2001 season ends with a crushing loss to the Rams, but within a couple of weeks Reeves, a 22-year head coach whose 189 victories rank No. 7 on the all-time NFL list, signs a new three-year contract.

His extension comes from a friendship with an owner who, like Michael Vick, is preparing for a rookie season of his own. Arthur Blank, believing Reeves to be far better than his 16-32 record, asks the coach to help him usher in a new era for the Falcons.

Blank, whose $545 million offer to buy the team was accepted by Rankin Smith's family on December 6, flew back with the team on the charter flight home from St. Louis. He wanted to know what the players were thinking as he considered the task before him.

The co-founder of The Home Depot understands the value of listening to customers, and will do no less for the Falcons. "If someone is thirsty, you give him something to drink," Blank says. "If someone is hungry, you give him something to eat."

And if this team has Michael Vick backing up Chris Chandler, Blank wants to do his part in what could be a year of change and self-discovery.

Arthur Blank offered Dan Reeves an opportunity to take the Falcons to the next level by extending his contract. Blank praised Reeves for both his work ethic and his ability to bring along young players. Reeves, the winningest active coach, knows the game as well as anyone in the league. He also knows that change is the norm in professional football and coaches must be able to adapt to survive in the pressure cooker called the NFL.

Lewis Grizzard, the late columnist for *The Atlanta Constitution*, urged readers in 1996 not to "forget that when the Atlanta Falcons entered the National Football League in the mid-'60s, they had a real live falcon as the team mascot." But the embarrassed bird "flew out of the stadium," Grizzard wrote, "never to return."

A BLANK SLATE—LIFE BEFORE ARTHUR

Dan Henning, above, won 35 percent of his games during a four-year stint as the Falcons coach. Norm Van Brocklin, below, has the longest tenure of any Falcons coach at seven seasons. His teams won 43 percent of their games from 1968 to 1974.

*I*t all began on August 1, 1966, when Wade Traynham whiffed on the first opening kickoff attempt in team history. With 20,072 watching in sparkling new Atlanta Stadium, the Falcons lost that first game 9-7 to the Philadelphia Eagles. It was an exhibition, a preseason contest that meant nothing. But, in a way, it set the tone for the ups and downs that make up the history of the Falcons.

According to local lore, Falcons founder Rankin Smith Sr., who owned the franchise until his death in 1997, wanted Vince Lombardi as Atlanta's first head coach. Lombardi expressed interest but wanted to become a minority owner. Smith rebuffed the Green Bay legend, then spoke with Hall of Famer Paul Brown. But Smith was worried Brown would be offended that Lombardi had been his first choice. He turned instead to Norb Hecker, the Packers secondary coach who compiled a 4-26-1 record and was fired after the Falcons began the '68 season 0-3.

GOOD CHEMISTRY BETWEEN COACHES AND PLAYERS IS AN ESSENTIAL INGREDIENT FOR A WINNING TEAM. HOW SUCCESSFULLY THE BOND IS FORMED IS VERY OFTEN THE MEASURE OF SUCCESS OR FAILURE IN PROFESSIONAL FOOTBALL.

In spite of everything, Atlanta's first draft in 1966 had been a success. Linebacker Tommy Nobis was taken No. 1 overall and terrorized the NFL until his knees finally forced him into retirement after the 1976 season. If any Falcon ever deserved to be in the Pro Football Hall of Fame—the team has never enshrined one of its own—Nobis was the man. But Atlanta's second draft in 1967 was a different story. Sixteen players from the '67 draft never touched the ball in a regular-season game—they just didn't have the stuff.

DUTCHMAN BRINGS THE HARD STUFF

After releasing Hecker, Smith turned to Norm Van Brocklin, legendary quarterback of the Los Angeles Rams and Philadelphia Eagles, as the Falcons next coach. From '68 through '71, "The Dutchman" owned a 19-31-3 record. Van

INTRODUCTION 19

Despite seasons of celebration and some exceptional players over the years, times weren't always the best for the Falcons.

Brocklin managed a few wins but his abrasive manner wasn't exactly promoting team spirit. His Falcons had their best season in 1973, going 9-5, but Van Brocklin was unemployed after the Falcons started 2-6 the following year. Atlanta's four-year run of sellout crowds ended after a 24-0 season-opening loss to Dallas in 1974. Few players or fans wept at Van Brocklin's departure.

SWAMP FOX HIT WITH PEPPLER SPRAY

Smith then gave the Falcons head coaching job to defensive coordinator Marion "Swamp Fox" Campbell, who was at least easier to get along with than Van Brocklin. By the time Campbell mopped up the remainder of the 1974 season with a 1-5 record, only 10,020 showed up to watch a meaningless win over Green Bay. The "Swamp Fox" moved on in 1976 after Smith reportedly told General Manager Pat Peppler, "You think you know so damn much, you go coach the team."

Peppler had never coached a football team on any level, explaining his 0-2 start and 59-0 setback in Los Angeles in early December.

AND SO IT WENT...

Dan Reeves was first interviewed by Smith in 1977, but 20 years and several more coaches would pass through Falcons portals before the Americus, Ga., native took the head coaching job.

The ship's next captain was Leeman Bennett. Atlanta's fifth head coach began his voyage in 1977, and the vessel sailed smoothly until January 5, 1981—the day Bennett went conservative on a 24-10 lead in Dallas and lost the game 30-27. Who could tell on that freezing night that the Falcons wouldn't host another playoff game for 18 years?

Though Bennett and General Manager Eddie LeBaron would both meet their demise in the 1980s, they were responsible for turning Atlanta into a pro football hotbed during their first four years together.

Bennett hired Jerry Glanville to coordinate a defense—the "Gritz Blitz"—that in 1977 set a modern-day NFL record by allowing only 129 total points in a 14-game season. Steve Bartkowski, the first quarterback Atlanta selected with a No. 1 overall pick, was a four-year starter in 1978 when he led the Falcons to a victory in their playoff debut. Two years later, Smith and everyone affiliated with the team enjoyed their finest ride. The Falcons went 12-4 and won the NFC West, their only division title in Smith's 32-year reign.

The following season, however, was a reality check. Despite placing seven players on the NFC Pro Bowl squad, the Falcons finished 7-9 with seven of their losses coming by an average of 2.7 points. Bennett was fired after the strike-shortened 1982 season.

Leeman Bennett led the Falcons to their first NFC West championship in 1980 and was fired two years later.

Whatever others may think, Reeves wants no part of portraying Rankin Smith Sr., or any of his family members as dispassionate or aloof. "They're great people to work for," Reeves says. "Anything I asked for, they gave me."

their next hire—Marion Campbell again. Winners such as Dick Vermeil, Terry Donahue, and Bill Parcells had left the Smiths standing at the altar. That '87 team finished last in points scored and last in points allowed.

Campbell lasted two and one-half seasons, then Jerry Glanville, the ol' Gritz Blitz coordinator, was next on the list. The bombastic, ego-driven Glanville lived a classic hard-livin', hard-hittin' NFL lifestyle, but he did coax a playoff season out of a four-year reign that ended in 1993.

HEY, A LOT OF PEOPLE COULDN'T SEE IT FROM OUR SIDE, BUT NOTHING HURT US WORSE THAN LOSING. MY DAD INCLUDED. HE WANTED TO WIN A SUPER BOWL FOR THIS CITY SO BADLY THAT HE DIDN'T MOVE THE FRANCHISE WHEN THAT OPPORTUNITY CAME UP AND HE COULD'VE MADE A LOT OF MONEY OFF THE DEAL.

MY DAD WAS FROM ATLANTA. HE LOVED ATLANTA. THE CITY AND THE PEOPLE HERE WERE ALWAYS GOOD TO US, AND WE TRIED TO RESPOND IN KIND. —TAYLOR SMITH

... AND WENT...

Former Washington offensive coordinator Dan Henning assumed the position of head coach in 1983. The Atlanta careers of Bartkowski, William Andrews, Alfred Jenkins, R.C. Thielemann, Jeff Van Note, Jeff Yeates, Tom Pridemore, Mike Pitts, and Kenny Johnson were waning.

Henning's arrival began a 19-year stretch in which the Falcons went 116-186 with only three winning records and as many playoff appearances. GM LeBaron's time ran out after the '85 season. Twelve years would pass before another general manager is hired.

... AND WENT

The Falcons fired Henning after an '86 season that began 5-1-1 and ended 7-8-1. Smith and Co. needed 43 days, an eternity in professional sports, to make their next hire—

Offensive coordinator June Jones was next on the block. Jones was the opposite of Glanville—soft-spoken almost to a fault. His 1995 Falcons went 9-7 and advanced to the playoffs. They also established an NFL record for passing yards allowed in a single season (4,751). Everything came unglued in the aftermath of a sideline confrontation when Jones pulled quarterback Jeff George in favor of Bobby Hebert during the third quarter of a blowout loss to Philadelphia at the half-filled Georgia Dome. George never took another snap for the Falcons, and Jones resigned at the end of a 3-13 campaign.

HOLD BACK THE DAWN

Dan Reeves finally arrived in 1997. In 1998 the Falcons shocked everyone by advancing to their first Super Bowl. Despite undergoing emergency quadruple bypass surgery in December of that year and sitting out three weeks, Reeves returned to orchestrate last-gasp playoff wins over San Francisco and Minnesota. But the team fell back into old habits and went 16-32 over the next three years.

There were rumblings in 2001. The organization was ripe for change—enter Michael Vick and Arthur Blank.

CHAPTER ONE

2.02.2002 FALCONS RECEIVE A BLANK CHECK

I PERSONALLY WILL NOT REST UNTIL I HAVE AN OPPORTUNITY TO WEAR A SUPER BOWL RING ON BEHALF OF EVERYBODY IN ATLANTA AND EVERYBODY IN THE STATE OF GEORGIA. THAT'S AN IMPORTANT GOAL OF MINE, AND I'LL TELL YOU THAT I'M NOT GOING TO REST UNTIL THAT TAKES PLACE. —ARTHUR BLANK

Arthur Blank's style is hands-on whether he's making deals with players, meeting with local officials, or making sure the fans are well taken care of.

*I*t's Feb. 2 in New Orleans. Outside, the air is cool and the sky dark blue on the day before St. Louis and New England will play in the Super Bowl.

Arthur Blank has run through his mental checklist time and time again. All is well, but those nagging thoughts won't let him rest. Having first expressed an interest in buying the Atlanta Falcons in the mid-'80s, Blank tries to quiet the inner doubts. Has he cleared every hurdle?

His meeting in New York on Jan. 23 with the NFL finance committee couldn't have gone better. All sides had practiced due diligence since Dec. 6, 2001, when the Smith family accepted Blank's offer to buy the Falcons for $545 million, and the finance committee had voted unanimously to bring Blank's name before all 32 owners on Super Bowl Eve. Only one committee member, Philadelphia Eagles owner Jeff Lurie,

> WE BUILT A GREAT COMPANY AT THE HOME DEPOT ON A VERY SIMPLE PHILOSOPHY. THE MORE I'M LEARNING ABOUT FOOTBALL, THE MORE I REALIZE THAT THE KEY PHILOSOPHY IS THE SAME. SURROUND YOURSELF WITH THE BEST PEOPLE. —ARTHUR BLANK

had been unable to fly to New York that day, but he sent a favorable proxy.

Chairman Al Lerner, owner of the Cleveland Browns, had been so kind. Blank's close friend, New England owner Robert Kraft, helped him relax. Blank could remember the looks on every committee member's face. Each owned an NFL franchise. The vote had been unanimous, yes, but even better was the feeling Blank had after he left the room.

He could tell the other owners—Tom

Benson of New Orleans, Lamar Hunt of Kansas City, Malcolm Glazer of Tampa Bay, Denver's Pat Bowlen, Tennessee's Bud Adams, and New York Giants Chairman Robert Tisch—wanted him to join their club. Blank knew NFL Commissioner Paul Tagliabue was eager to tap into Blank's wealth of resources.

When he finally enters the Inter-Continental Hotel conference room in New Orleans, Blank can sense an optimistic buzz. Any fears are assuaged when the 32 owners, from Oakland's Al

Continued on page 27

There are probably no two bigger supporters of the state of Georgia than Arthur Blank and former President Jimmy Carter, seen here before the Falcons 30-3 win over Cincinnati on Sept. 22, 2002.

CHAPTER **ONE**   25

THE ARTHUR BLANK STORY

BLANK INTENDS TO EXTEND HIS EXPERIENCE AND VALUES TO THE FALCONS, BUILDING BOTH A COMPETITIVELY AND FINANCIALLY SUCCESSFUL FRANCHISE—AND GIVING SOMETHING BACK TO ATLANTA.

Arthur Blank's outlook on life is simple. "We are nothing if we don't act on our beliefs," he says. "Our family believes in doing what's necessary to go to the mountain top, but then to return to the community and put our ideas into action." Though he soon turns 61, Blank still runs about 20 miles a week. The man whose adopted life motto—"There Is No Finish Line"—has competed in nearly 500 runs, including five marathons.

LEARNING LIFE'S LESSONS

Born in Flushing, N.Y., and raised in Queens, Arthur is the younger of Max and Molly Blank's two sons. His father, who owned a struggling pharmaceutical company, died of a heart attack at age 40.

Fifteen-year-old Arthur and his brother Michael watched as their mother gave up her sculpting career to take charge of the family business, which she transformed into a successful company that she sold in the 1970s. "I guess I did OK," she told the *Los Angeles Times* in January 1999.

Molly Blank didn't just teach each of her sons how to run a

Arthur and Stephanie Blank extend their concept of family into the Atlanta community. They are both active supporters of worthy causes while centering much of what they do around their children. Giving something back is a credo both embrace with gusto.

DURING BLANK'S 23 YEARS WITH THE HOME DEPOT, THE COMPANY DONATED MORE THAN $113 MILLION TO COMMUNITIES, AND HOME DEPOT ASSOCIATES PROVIDED HUNDREDS OF THOUSANDS OF HOURS OF PERSONAL VOLUNTEER TIME.

successful business; she also instilled a belief in being "our brother's keeper" and investing in one's community. She showed the boys how to practice and live the tenants of Judaism and required a focus on family as well. "I center a lot of things I do around my family, says Blank. He has three adult children, Kenny, Dena and Danielle, who sit on the board of trustees of the family foundation. Together, Arthur and Stephanie, his second wife, have three youngsters, 6-year-old Joshua and 18-month-old twins Kylie and Max. Spending time with all of the children is Arthur and Stephanie's top priority.

STEWARDSHIP AND SERVICE ARE ENDURING GOALS

Blank readily admits that football, baseball, and track took precedence over academics in high school. A knee injury suffered as a receiver-defensive back in his junior year in high school ended Blank's football career. But he used that setback as a chance to improve himself in other areas, making the dean's list all four years at Babson College where he developed a life-long passion for golf.

Along the way he has never forgotten his mother's lessons about stewardship and service. When he and Stephanie were married in 1995 they requested that guests make donations to Outward Bound in lieu of wedding presents.

ALL OR NOTHING

Arthur Blank is a man who has high expectations of those around him and and even higher expectations of himself. "That's the thing about Mr. B, he doesn't settle for anything but the best," says Bob Whitfield, the Falcons long-time offensive lineman who knows a little about excellence himself.

Bringing in top-end advisors at every level of the game is just good business sense. Former 49ers quarterback Steve Young and Blank talk things over at a Falcons practice.

Continued from page 25

Davis to Dallas' Jerry Jones, all vote yes.

The actual sale of the Falcons won't close until Feb. 13, but Arthur Blank finally can look in the mirror and see an NFL owner.

RUNNING START

From the minute he starts speaking at a news conference held at the Inter-Continental, Blank begins laying out a business plan for the Falcons based on the same principles he used to co-found The Home Depot in 1978. He and Bernie Marcus had turned the Atlanta-based company into the world's largest home improvement retailer. Surely he could rebuild the Falcons. Right?

Well, if anyone can transform the team, Blank is the man. Before he and Marcus opened their company, no operator in the do-it-yourself warehouse industry had reported a profit in a financial quarter. Home Depot rocketed through the marketplace by selling merchandise at low prices and training managers and store clerks to treat all customers with respect.

Blank and Marcus opened their first two stores in 1979. Twenty years later, they had 930. Plans called for over 1500 by the end of 2002. The Home Depot reached $1 billion in sales in 1987 and passed $50 billion in 2001.

Dan Reeves presents Arthur Blank with the game ball following the Falcons 30-3 victory over Cincinnati to commemorate the owner's first regular-season win.

"We built a great company at Home Depot on a very simple philosophy," Blank said. "The more I'm learning about football and about the Falcons and the NFL, the more I realize that the key philosophy is the same. That is, you hire the very best people. Surround yourself with the best people."

CHAPTER ONE 27

The Falcons need a major renovation, but John Imlay thinks the odds are in Blank's favor. Imlay, an Atlanta venture capitalist who owned 6 percent of the team under the Smith family, has bought back 1.67 percent of the franchise, paying approximately $9 million in March 2002.

"Arthur is the most organized person I've ever dealt with," Imlay says. "This is a demanding effort he's undertaken, but he has great ability to delegate. I feel he'll fill all his commitments, meet some expectations, and even surpass some."

As chairman, president, and CEO of the Falcons, Blank immediately starts delegating responsibility. His first major hire is executive vice president of marketing Dick Sullivan, the former senior vice president of marketing at Home Depot.

When plans to hire former Green Bay Packers executive VP and general manager Ron Wolf fall through, Blank turns to Bobby Beathard as his senior advisor. Beathard, having worked 37 years in the NFL, doesn't want the GM job in Atlanta. But he agrees to come out of retirement after discussing his role with Blank and former Washington coach Joe Gibbs, a NASCAR team owner who joined Imlay and apartment properties developer John Williams as a minority investor in the Falcons. Beathard worked more than a decade as the Redskins GM, ending in May 1989, and another decade as San Diego GM, ending in April 2000.

Blank is finding out that an NFL owner wears a lot of hats. But whether he's on television with Jerry Jones, talking with his head coach, or listening to his players, the future of the Falcons is always on his mind.

28   ATLANTA FALCONS

> WE CAN CREATE A BETTER GAME DAY EXPERIENCE FOR OUR FANS. PART OF THAT OBVIOUSLY IS HAVING A WINNING TEAM. IT GOES BEYOND THAT. THE GAME DAY EXPERIENCE CONSISTS OF EVERYTHING FROM SELLING A TICKET, TO PARKING, TO THE GEORGIA DOME EXPERIENCE, AND CREATING THAT NFL EXPERIENCE EVERY SINGLE TIME WE PLAY FOOTBALL AT THE GEORGIA DOME. —ARTHUR BLANK

Ray Anderson comes on as EVP and chief administrative officer. Dan Reeves is executive vice president and head coach. Ron Hill signs a two-year contract extension in September 2002 to remain vice president of football operations. Susan Bass is hired to oversee community and public relations and Greg Beadles is promoted as vice president of finance.

Blank's newly appointed board of directors consists of Imlay, Gibbs, Williams, Atlanta Olympics organizer Billy Payne, former U.N. ambassador and Atlanta mayor Andrew Young, Coca-Cola chief of public affairs Carl Ware, former Falcons quarterback Steve Bartkowski, developer John Aderhold, Bennett College president Johnetta Cole, long time financial advisor David Homrich, and investment advisor Felker Ward.

After agreeing to contract terms with Reeves, Blank challenges him to surround himself with the best and signs off on the coach's desire to hire Wade Phillips as defensive coordinator, Emmitt Thomas as secondary coach, Ollie Wilson to coach running backs, and Mike Johnson to coach receivers.

"I will tell you that I personally will not rest until I have an opportunity to wear a Super Bowl ring on behalf of everybody in Atlanta and everybody in the state of Georgia," Blank says. "That's an important goal of mine, and I'll tell you that I'm not going to rest until that takes place."

CHAPTER ONE

IMMEDIATE DIVIDENDS

Blank sees immediate dividends for long-suffering fans. Though he declines to be specific two weeks after his acceptance into the league, Blank has big changes in store for game days.

"I think we're very fortunate in that every discussion I've had with the folks at the Georgia Dome has been positive," Blank says. "They have been very open. They want it to be a great game-day experience for the fans. They've seen what happens during the Southeastern Conference championship game inside the Dome. In my opinion, that's the way it can be every single Sunday. We can bring that level of excitement."

As a former Falcons season-ticket holder, Blank knows he is taking charge of a team that has never consistently filled the Dome, a state-owned building.

Even Atlanta's thrilling 20-18 victory over San Francisco in the playoffs on Jan. 9, 1999, was 1000 short of the crowd numbers that annually attend the SEC championship and the Peach Bowl in the Dome.

ATLANTA FALCONS

Filling the seats at the Georgia Dome for every game is Blank's goal. To do that he must put a winner on the field and in the front office.

I THINK WE'RE VERY FORTUNATE IN THAT EVERY DISCUSSION I'VE HAD WITH THE FOLKS AT THE GEORGIA DOME HAS BEEN POSITIVE. —ARTHUR BLANK

CREATING GAME-DAY EXCITEMENT

"I think the beauty of this is that there are some things I think we can fix almost immediately," Blank says. "Some of them might take a little more time.

"We can create a better game-day experience for our fans. Part of that obviously is having a winning team. It goes beyond that. The game day experience consists of everything from selling a ticket, to parking, to the Georgia Dome experience, and creating that NFL experience every single time we play football at the Georgia Dome."

Very few people in the history of Atlanta sports could have changed the complexion of the Falcons in a few months, but Blank believes in customer satisfaction. Arthur has a plan, and he's sticking to it.

CHAPTER ONE   31

ARTHUR BELIEVES IN ATLANTA

Community service is Arthur Blank's passion. Giving something back to the city he loves goes beyond writing checks and attending charity events. Arthur Blank is committed to Atlanta and Atlanta is committed to him.

On Feb. 15, 2002, a few days after closing on his purchase of the team, Blank sits in his office overlooking the Falcons practice fields. A year has passed since he retired from The Home Depot, resigning as CEO and leaving the company's board of directors.

Many people at his age fortunate enough to be billionaires might sail off into the sunset, but Blank only dives deeper into philanthropy and takes on more responsibilities.

Arthur Blank's legacy is easy to define. His generous gifts have already left a lasting impression in the Atlanta community. He spearheads capital campaigns for the Atlanta Symphony Orchestra's new concert hall and a museum to commemorate the 1996 Olympics. He's a founding and current trustee of The Carter Center and maintains directorships with Staples and Cox Enterprises.

He is currently chairman of the Metro Atlanta Chamber of Commerce, an Emory University trustee, and a distinguished executive in residence at the business school. In addition he oversees an investment firm that bears his name.

HOW MUCH IS ENOUGH?

The question is—how much attention can he give the Falcons? "I've got to work all that through and try to reassess every place I'm spending my time today and try to make some adjustments," Blank says. "Because I certainly want to have time with my family, for all of my children, and for my personal health."

Blank may still be figuring out how to juggle all the balls, but one thing is clear there are no boundaries on his interest in community service. What separates Blank

Blank takes to the microphone at halftime to raise money for worthy causes such as the Atlanta Symphony Orchestra. Enhancing cultural experiences in Atlanta is a priority for Blank and his family's foundation.

from many donors is his ability to listen and a willingness to respond with a kind of grace that makes those receiving his help feel special. He has the gift of instilling dignity as he offers a helping hand.

INVOLVED ON AND OFF THE FIELD

The Arthur M. Blank Family Foundation has given more than $100 million to local and national non-profits serving the arts, education, environment and

Arthur Blank's legacy is easy to define. His generous gifts have already left a lasting impression in the Atlanta community.

Arthur Blank spends some quality time at a computer with Georgia's next generation as former 49ers quarterback Steve Young looks on. He sets the example by his actions and expects community involvement and commitment from every Falcons associate.

youth development.

The Atlanta Falcons Youth Foundation is a now a fund of Blank's family foundation, and focuses on physical fitness, athletics and team building for Georgia's young people. The Youth Foundation awarded more than $1 million in grants and scholarships last year, and is set to double that amount in 2003.

TEAM OUTREACH

Under Blank's leadership, the team's community outreach efforts are grounded in the goals of the Youth Foundation and involve the entire Falcons organization. Players, coaches, and staff give back through donations of time and money to schools and community groups throughout the state of Georgia. The Atlanta Falcons Spouses Association also participates by raising funds and awareness for organizations that serve women and children.

CHAPTER TWO

VICK

2.25.02—MICHAEL'S THE MAN

Sitting at home in Virginia a few days after Chris Chandler is released, Michael Vick is getting a little stir crazy. The Falcons off-season conditioning program won't begin until April 2, but the heir apparent needs to channel his energy—and with good reason. The regular season may be months away, but to Vick it's just around the corner.

With Chandler's release on Feb. 25, Vick becomes Atlanta's starting quarterback. His mind is racing as he calls his position coach, Jack Burns, who encourages him to "come down and let's talk about some things."

Days later, Vick is pacing the hallways of the Falcons complex, ready to watch some tape.

"Man, I had to do something," he says. "There's so much I want to do, so much to accomplish. I've still got so much to learn."

He and Burns schedule a meeting with Reeves the following Monday to discuss the intricacies of Atlanta's encyclopedia-size playbook.

"He was telling me they have been working on ways to cut down on some of the verbiage," Vick says. "A lot of the problems I had, though, were mistakes

When people talk about me, I want them to smile. That's why I try to do so many things in the community. It's not just about me. I have what I want, but I want to have an impact on other people and be able to do good things for them. —Michael Vick

RETOOLING THE PLAYBOOK

that I made. Nothing to do with the players around me. Things I can control."

Even for a super star athlete with a $63 million contract, the off-season has been draining. Old friends constantly call. Most just want a piece of his time. Others offer ways to spend his money.

Returning to the team complex helps Vick relax. But with Chandler gone after five years as Atlanta's starter, Vick feels the weight of responsibility.

"He was great for me, a great teacher and a leader," Vick says. "He taught me so much."

Chandler, about to sign a contract with the Chicago Bears, has fond memories of his relationship with Vick.

"He always showed me a lot of respect, and that's what made it—I believe—as easy as it could be," Chandler says in a telephone interview. "He didn't have any control over the way fans act or react. He was always in my corner, and he is a really good kid. I really wish him the best.

"It's going to be fun down the road to hopefully see him turn into the player everyone wants him to be and thinks he can be. Now it's going to be a long, hard road still, but when I am done playing, it'll be fun to sit back and watch him."

A NEW BREED OF ATHLETE

In his next life, Michael Vick wants to float like a butterfly and sting like a bee.

"I'm a big-time boxing fan," he says. "I'm crazy over boxing."

Vick and a few friends are sitting in the den of his Duluth, Ga., home on the night of March 1, 2003. The room buzzes

Continued on page 41

*E*ric Zeier always had the mind of a quarterback. When the Falcons traded for him in March 2001, Zeier was a six-year NFL veteran who set 18 Southeastern Conference and 67 school records in a University of Georgia career that ended in 1994.

His father, Army sergeant Rick Zeier, groomed the boy to understand the essentials of passing routes and coverage schemes. Eric was good enough to start 12 of his 26 games for Cleveland, Baltimore, and Tampa Bay. Atlanta acquired him to compete with Doug Johnson for the No. 2 job behind Chris Chandler.

Zeier, who would be cut by the end of preseason, entered his first meeting with Chandler, Johnson, and quarterbacks coach Jack Burns, eager to get a feel for the Falcons playbook.

"The first time they called a play, I was like, 'Whoa. Come again?'" Zeier said. "They were talking in another language."

Chandler's arrival in a 1997 trade with the Houston Oilers had taken Atlanta's offense to a more complicated level. This guy was highly intelligent. Difficulties Chandler encountered in the Falcons locker room, which were many, resulted from a tendency to brood.

Grasping the intricacies of a game plan, however, was like counting to 10 for Chandler. The longer he played for the Falcons, the more layers Reeves added to the playbook.

Agility, speed, intelligence, and great improvisational skills—what more could you ask of a franchise-saving quarterback? Maybe the Super Bowl?

TOUGH TRANSITION

NFL coaches have long maintained an adage that a quarterback's biggest jump in awareness comes between the first and second years. Michael Vick was no exception.

His rookie year included a variety of struggles at the line of scrimmage and in the huddle. Vick often called the wrong formations and wrong protections, or he'd see the defense make changes as he got ready to take a snap and draw a blank.

Trouble was on the way.

"What used to happen is I'd get in the huddle, and Dan would give the play to me through the headset, and I'm saying it to myself so I can have a picture of the play in my mind," Vick said. "I didn't want to get in the huddle and say the play and then get to the line and then have to create a picture of the play in my mind.

"At the same time, I'm looking at the hash (mark) we're on, looking at the defense, seeing what personnel they've substituted in and all that. And then I'd forget the play!"

Johnson could see both sides of the situation. By his second season in 2001, Johnson had attended enough meetings and practices to make the necessary transition. He understood the Atlanta playbook no matter how complicated it was.

On the other hand, Johnson saw a need for simplification. He came to the Falcons as an undrafted college free agent

Continued on page 40

CHAPTER **TWO**

VICKTORIOUS

ATLANTA FALCONS

CHAPTER TWO 39

Continued from page 37

from Florida. Reeves and Burns were impressed with his arm strength and with the fact that he played for coach Steve Spurrier, whose Gators ran one of the NCAA's most prolific offenses.

"At Florida, when we got in the huddle to call a play, the quarterback said just one number," Johnson said. "That told everybody what to do and where to go."

HELP ON THE WAY

When the Falcons decided in late February 2002 that Vick would be their starter, Reeves charged his assistants with revising the playbook. The coaching staff wanted to reduce the verbiage and streamline the offense, not just for their 22-year-old quarterback, but for rookies and newcomers too.

Reeves, who broke into the NFL as a reserve running back for Dallas in 1965, still ran an offense based on principles he learned as a longtime player, assistant coach, and coordinator under Cowboys coach Tom Landry. The fundamentals of the playbook were still sound, but at 58 and about to enter his 22nd year as a head coach, Reeves had no intention of laboring several months to make it adapt to the new century.

"Hey, I know how to open my e-mail," Reeves said, smiling broadly. The same could be said for the 53-year-old Burns, who described himself as "not what you'd call a computer expert."

On the other hand, special teams coach Joe DeCamillis began to see football in a Windows world during Reeves' 1993-96 tenure with the New York Giants. DeCamillis, Reeves' 38-year-old son-in-law, had one of the NFL's better special teams units the past three years—primarily because of his players, but digital game plans haven't hurt.

Offensive line coach Pete Mangurian and receivers coach Mike Johnson have readily embraced change too. Mangurian, 47, worked under Reeves in Denver and New York, and joined the Atlanta staff before working from 1998 to 2000 as head coach at Cornell. During his time in Ithaca, N.Y., Mangurian learned how to use spreadsheets and data processing to his advantage, and he wanted the Falcons to upgrade their system when he returned in January 2001.

Johnson, 35, had similar experience as quarterbacks coach of the San Diego Chargers in 2000-01. The ability of software to introduce plays visually and the ability to make tweaks to suit a team's personnel would make a positive impact.

Mangurian converted the running game, Johnson the passing attack. They worked with Reeves, Burns, and other staff members to make the offense fit the team. Vick wasn't just relieved. He was energized too.

"It made a huge difference," Vick said in March 2003. "I think it helped everybody and it made us a better team." At the same time, Vick hadn't exactly reached a Zen level of simplification. He grinned when asked in training camp to give the etymology of one play.

"OK, (in 2001) you might go, 'Pass, seven, deep, flat, king, left, trips, Z, shades, D2, 35, quarterback, pass, wing, 8Y6,' " Vick said.

And now?

"This year it's just, 'King, left, trips, flame, 5, 515, 6, 8.' " Flowery Branch wasn't built in a day.

Continued from page 36

with debate about the fighter's skills.

As the undercard ends, Vick joins the camp of John Ruiz, who will make his first defense of the WBA heavyweight title he earned after beating Evander Holyfield. The challenger, Roy Jones Jr., is trying to become the first light heavyweight champion to win a heavyweight title since Michael Spinks beat Larry Holmes in 1985.

Ruiz, 31, is 3 years younger, 3 inches taller, and 23 pounds heavier than Jones, who has never fought in the top division. Las Vegas oddsmakers side with Jones' boxing skills and brush off the fact that Ruiz's reach is 7 inches longer. Jones, who can become the first former middleweight champ to win a heavyweight title since 1897, is a 9-5 favorite.

"Well, I thought Ruiz was going to beat him because he's just so much bigger," Vick says two weeks later. Leaning forward on the edge of his sofa, Vick is getting excited. "But then I see an interview with Roy Jones, and he says, 'I'm a new breed of athlete. I do things that other people can't do.' My feet movement is like Ali's. I can see three punches before he can see my one," Vick says of Jones.

"What he was saying, and the reason I say that, is that he has talent no one else has. After I saw this interview I said, 'Roy Jones is going to win this fight. He's going to beat him in 12 rounds, and Ruiz ain't going to touch Roy.' "

> THE GUYS WHO PLAY THE GAME FOR THE LOVE ARE THE ONES THAT GO TO THE SUPER BOWL; JERRY RICE, EMMITT SMITH, GUYS WHO WANT TO BE SUCCESSFUL. —MICHAEL VICK

Jones wins a unanimous 12-round decision, and Vick is very excited.

CHANGING THE WAY THE THE GAME IS PLAYED

How many football players are good enough to play quarterback in the NFL? Of those, how many have the poise and talent to win a starting job? And of those, how many are fast and strong enough to set three league records for rushing by a quarterback?

"That's why I understand why people get so excited about some of the things I do," Vick says. "I've been blessed. Roy Jones has been blessed."

Throughout 2002, as the media searched for ways to describe Vick's sensational ability, "new breed of quarterback" is one label that stuck.

Well, yes and no.

Most people agree that Michael Vick is unlike any quarterback that's come before him. To say he's the first of a new generation of quarterbacks, however, suggests that others like him will follow.

No chance, says Deion Sanders.

Sanders was a similar one-of-a-kind talent when the Falcons drafted him No. 5 overall in 1989 out of Florida State. Here was a cornerback and return specialist who would change the way the game is played. Sanders became the first athlete ever to play in a Super Bowl (1994 with San Francisco, '95 with Dallas) and a World Series (1992 with the Atlanta Braves).

For most of his 12 years in the NFL, nobody covered receivers and returned kickoffs and punts like Sanders. And nobody, before or after he retired in 2000, remotely resembled the man who called himself "Prime Time."

Sanders sees so much of himself in Vick.

"It seems like the game slows down when he's running, like everybody's running half-speed—and they're not. They're running at full speed," says Sanders, who worked in 2002 as an NFL studio analyst for CBS. "He's just that much faster, and he has vision. That's what people don't understand. His vision while running the ball is unbelievable, and it goes unmentioned.

"He's a game breaker and he's a game

changer. I mean there are a lot of great players in the NFL, but there ain't but a couple of game changers. This guy changed the game. A few people have come along in life in the game of football that change your perception of the game. It challenges college coaches to go and recruit, scouts to go and look for this type of player. And that's what he's done. That's a game changer, not a game breaker."

Sanders loves Vick's willingness to play the game with unbridled joy.

"That's exactly the way it should be," Sanders says. "Just because we're adults, people tend to want to, you know, measure you to be like a grown man, and there's no such thing. People forget football is a game. Game is the key word."

Vick is constantly approached by well-wishers, Falcons fans or not, who tell him how much they appreciate the way his physical skills affect his spirit, and vice versa.

"When people think about me, they don't put me in a category with John Elway or Joe Montana," Vick says. "Maybe the way I play with emotion or my love for the game, but not my style of play. You know, I'm not a drop-back passer. I'm not a running quarterback. I'm both. I do things a little different."

RUNS IN THE FAMILY

Vick's second cousin, New Orleans quarterback Aaron Brooks, begins the season with a 2-1 career record against the Falcons, but he and the Saints will lose both games against Atlanta. After Vick refuses to relent and the Falcons beat the Saints 37-35 on a last-second field goal at the Louisiana Superdome, Brooks is amazed.

"He has revolutionized the game," Brooks says.

Vick loves competing against a relative who always seemed just out of reach. Brooks, who's four years older, went to Ferguson High School and Vick went to Warwick in their hometown of Newport News, Va. The year Michael finally made it to high school, Brooks was a world away in Charlottesville learning the nuances of university life.

Every time Vick closed the gap on his cousin, Brooks seemed to take another step out of reach. Vick made it to college in 1998 and was a redshirt freshman at Virginia Tech when Brooks led the Virginia Cavaliers to one of the greatest comebacks in school history—a 36-32 win over the Hokies. Brooks had 345 yards passing and three second-half touchdown strikes. Vick stood and watched.

> WHEN PEOPLE THINK ABOUT ME, THEY DON'T PUT ME IN A CATEGORY WITH JOHN ELWAY OR JOE MONTANA. MAYBE THE WAY I PLAY WITH EMOTION OR MY LOVE FOR THE GAME, BUT NOT MY STYLE OF PLAY. YOU KNOW, I'M NOT A DROP-BACK PASSER. I'M NOT A RUNNING QUARTERBACK. I'M BOTH. I DO THINGS A LITTLE DIFFERENT. —MICHAEL VICK

In 1999, the acclaim Brooks reached on the state level soon would pale in comparison to Vick's accomplishments on a national scale. Brooks, a fourth-round draft pick for the Green Bay Packers that year, was third on the depth chart behind Brett Favre and Matt Hasselbeck when Vick took over as the starter at Virginia Tech and became the most exciting player in college football.

Leading the Hokies to an undefeated regular season, Vick helped Virginia Tech advance to the national championship game against Florida State at the Superdome. The Seminoles won 46-29, but Vick passed for 225 yards, ran for 97, and created a buzz that would surround him and Virginia Tech throughout 2000.

He had been named Big East Rookie of the Year and Offensive Player of the Year, becoming the first player in any conference to win both awards in the same season.

After setting an NCAA record for passing efficiency by a freshman (180.4 rating), Vick became the first freshman to be invited to the Heisman Trophy ceremony since the event was first televised in 1981.

Vick's sophomore season never matched the hype of the previous year. Virginia Tech was ranked No. 2 and unbeaten when it traveled to Miami in 2000. But Vick had a severely sprained right ankle and the Hokies, who had lost nine starters from their dominating defense the year before, were unmasked in a 41-21 loss.

Meanwhile in New Orleans, Brooks had been traded from Green Bay and was working as the No. 2 quarterback. He took charge of the Saints offense after starter Jeff Blake was lost for the season in late November. With a 3-2 record the rest of the way, Brooks played well enough to help New Orleans win the first division title in franchise history.

The Saints beat defending Super Bowl champion St. Louis at the Superdome in the wild card round of the playoffs as Brooks passed for 266 yards and four touchdowns. Brooks was the toast of the town.

Though Vick was the NFL's No. 1 overall draft pick in 2001, he stood on the sideline both times the Falcons played New Orleans. The Atlanta defense stopped Brooks and running back Ricky Williams in the second half of the first game, a 20-13 Falcons victory, but Brooks and Co. won the sequel convincingly at the Georgia Dome.

Last year's trip to New Orleans marked the first time that Vick and Brooks, who are related through marriages on their mothers' sides, played an organized football game on the same field.

"There's not that much of a difference, except that he's much, much, much faster," Brooks says. "Teams have to account for him in terms of his speed and what he can do outside of the pocket. With myself, I'm trying to pick a defense apart."

Though Vick made some breathtaking plays to beat the Saints twice in 2002, he has only praise for his cousin.

"It's an amazing story," Vick says. "Both of us had that work ethic, and we wanted it. Both of us set our goal to make it to the NFL. I've watched him throughout his career. He's had his ups and downs. My path has been a little different from his. But regardless of that, we started in the same place, we had the same dream, and we made it out."

NO LABELS ALLOWED

On this overcast day in mid-March, after discussing his love for boxing, Vick settles back into the comfort of the beige sofa in his living room. He can't wait for the season to start. He also wants another three months away from the game.

Michael Vick does not live in a black-and-white world. Try to label him and he sidesteps an observer the same way he avoids an oncoming blitz.

He loves hip-hop, yet he's an avid fisherman. He grew up in the Ridley Circle housing project of Newport News, but his Atlanta "crib" sits in a gated community among other top-dollar estate homes.

Knowing he was entering 2002 as the starter, Vick took some time for reflection at his 15-acre country home near the Chesapeake Bay, where he and his closest friends fire up the grill, pack the cooler, tell old stories, and laugh all night.

"There's a lake around the corner we've been going to, and you can go deep-sea fishing just 15 minutes away," Vick says. "I've got all my four-wheelers, my jet-skis out there, and it's about 40 minutes away from my mom."

Vick grew up in a tough neighborhood. His family always provided a buffer for the societal pitfalls that doom so many. Brenda Vick Boddie, his mother, and Michael Boddie, his father, married, then separated but always maintained a relationship. Vick, the couple's second child and oldest son, credits the Boys and Girls Clubs of Hampton Roads with providing a critical after-school haven of sorts from first grade through middle school.

He knows his family won't face similar obstacles. Someday his family will hear how their father became a millionaire at 20. They'll hear about the hardships the family once had and how they should appreciate everything around them.

ENJOYING THE REWARDS

"It almost seems unreal that you can have anything you want," Vick says. "It makes you appreciate life and appreciate all the things it took to get here. That makes it even sweeter. All the time and dedication and the hard work that you put in, you can make it pay off. It's a good feeling.

"I had a hard time growing up, but my mom had a job. My dad had a job. It was never enough, but we always

Continued on page 48

After Chris Chandler's release on Feb. 25, 2002, Vick moved from backup to starter. To make the adjustment easier for Vick, the other rookies, and newcomers, Reeves and the coaching staff began retooling the playbook. The goal was to simplify play calling to eliminate confusion on the field. Football is a learning process for everyone involved.

DAN REEVES

Hopefully I'm perceived as a guy who's doing the best job he possibly can to turn this team around. I appreciate

Pete Mangurian, right, a longtime line coach under Reeves, is promoted to offensive coordinator after the 2002 team finishes fourth in rushing. Wade Phillips, bottom, worked as defensive coordinator under Reeves in Denver before returning in the same capacity with Atlanta in January 2002.

*R*evising the Falcons playbook to accommodate Michael Vick was a major step for Coach Dan Reeves. But he took a bigger leap of faith by freeing Vick to improvise after the snap. Everyone is surprised when Vick puts on a dazzling display of skills and poise in the 2002 season opener at Green Bay. The game plan allows him to freelance—when necessary he can run for the score or he can dump a short pass.

It shows that Reeves can adapt. He's tough. He's a survivor. It's no accident that he begins 2003 with 197 career victories—ranking No. 7 all-time—because he knows how to change with the times.

"I don't think Dan gets enough credit for the work he's done with Mike," Blank says. "He's shown tremendous resolve here in working with younger players, older players, those from different cultures and all walks of life."

For Reeves, the road to success is paved with hard work, and he intends to honor his contract and coach the Falcons through 2004, if not longer.

"Hopefully, I'm perceived as a guy who's doing the best job he possibly can to get this team turned around," Reeves says six weeks into the 2002 season.

Reeves believes the only way he can

COACHING MICHAEL
Arthur giving me the chance because we really aren't where we want to be. —Dan Reeves

succeed is with results, not promises. And, he doesn't live in the past.

"I don't think you can worry about that as a coach," he says. "As long as you can look yourself in the mirror every day and say, 'Hey, I'm doing the best job I can.' I think I'm doing exactly that. Certainly we can improve on what we're doing, but we're working hard."

> ALL THE TIME AND DEDICATION AND THE HARD WORK THAT YOU PUT IN, YOU CAN MAKE IT PAY OFF. IT'S A GOOD FEELING. —MICHAEL VICK

Continued from page 45

seemed to have what we needed. I had family around me to support me and keep me away from things that other people got caught up in. I was fortunate, very fortunate—me and my little brother. Just living where I was living, that's when I realized that if I didn't do something or my brother didn't do something or my mom and dad didn't do something, we'd probably still be living in the same projects we were living in. That's when I set goals for myself.

"The day I got drafted No. 1 overall it was just so unreal—an unbelievable experience."

BRING IT ON

Vick fully embraces the burden of responsibility. He can't comprehend how a talented player such as Ryan Leaf, the quarterback San Diego chose No. 2 overall in 1998, allowed a less than perfect attitude to sabotage a promising career.

"The guys who play the game for the love are the ones who go to the Super Bowl—Jerry Rice, Emmitt Smith, guys who want to be successful," Vick says. "Some guys just don't care. What he did, I couldn't have done that."

"And for my career to be done in four years? Never, ever. I love the game too much. When you go out there on Sundays, you represent a lot of people."

Like any employee of any company, Vick hardly agrees with everything his coaches and teammates say. He admits he can be stubborn at times. Some of them say he could do a better job of listening. Ultimately, though, Vick intends to leave a legacy of hard work, integrity, and championships.

"I put myself in a situation like when I was a kid and I used to look at Michael Jordan," Vick says. "I know now I've got kids the same way. When you're a professional, people look at you like you're special. When people and kids look at me, I want them to know I'm a good person. I'm down to earth. I do whatever it takes to be successful.

"When people talk about me, I want them to smile. That's why I try to do so many things in the community. It's not just about me. I have what I want, but I want to have an impact on other people and be able to do good things for them."

CHAPTER **TWO** 49

CHAPTER THREE
TRAINING CAMP

Training camp is about focus and determination. If you're a rookie it's about making the team, if you're a veteran it's about keeping your job. Practices are hard, demanding work under the hot southern sun.

Beginning July 24, 2003, the Falcons will hold training camp for the fifth straight sweltering year at Furman University in Greenville, S.C. Nobody tells a better story of his training camp experience than left tackle Bob Whitfield, the longest-tenured Falcon and one of the funniest players ever to wear an Atlanta uniform.

Whitfield, the team's No. 8 overall draft pick in 1992 and a durable pro whose 172 games rank fourth in team history, is sitting on a sofa in an upstairs loft of his downtown Atlanta studio, PatchWerk Recordings. With four months remaining before the start of training camp, the 6-foot-5, 310-pound Whitfield has other topics he'd rather discuss.

Like lunch, for example.

> To survive at training camp is going against that one man and then beating him again the next day. So if he's tired and he's getting worn down mentally, then you have an advantage. —Bob Whitfield

The Falcons are no different from other clubs that open training camp in late July. Practices are tough but teams must ensure their players take regular breaks from the oppressive heat. At Furman University the temperature reaches 94 degrees with a heat index of 99. Reeves says, "we're monitoring the heat index, making sure they've got plenty of water, checking them between practices and replenishing fluids."

Reporter: *So about training camp?*

Big Whit: Training camp? OK, training camp. Well, physically you know what to expect. You've got to get up early as hell. Breakfast at 8, practice starts at 9. Train for 2 to 2½ hours, go to lunch. Hopefully, you're not hurting and have to go to treatment at 1 o'clock. Take a nap, then back at practice at 3. Go to dinner, get like 30 minutes to yourself, and then go to night meetings. Then grab a snack and back to your room and fall asleep at 11.

The Falcons Ball Boy Mentoring Program for disadvantaged kids starts at training camp and goes through the entire season.

CHAPTER **THREE**   51

Reporter: *Is there a sense of dread that overcomes you when you think about that part of the year?*

Big Whit: What makes training camp hard is not the activities you have to do or the expectations placed on you, it's the person you have to go against. I don't care if you're going against a Pro Bowler, first-teamer, rookie or scout team, whatever he has to offer that's what you go against. There's nothing else. To survive at training camp is going against that one man and then beating him again the next day. So if he's tired and he's getting worn down mentally, then you have an advantage. If he's making mistakes mentally, then you make it through training camp. That's how it can be a breeze. If you're looking at it as, 'Oh, (shoot). We're here for four (freakin') weeks,' then you get all bogged down on the (stuff).

Reporter: *When you were a rookie, did you feel like you had to make a good impression as soon as camp started?*

Big Whit: You still do that. Yeah, when you first get in the league, you think you're trying to prove it to them, but as you get older, you know you're just proving it to yourself. It ain't about them anymore. It ain't about improving my resume or improving my standing. I'm proving it to myself. If you take pride in being a professional and you take pride in being successful and take pride in whupping the (stuff) out of somebody, you ain't doing it for them no more. You're doing it for yourself, and they just reap the benefits from that.

ATLANTA FALCONS

Everybody gets tired. It's a mental thing, and you tell yourself not to let yourself drag. You know if you need to sprint, then you better sprint. If it's OK to jog, then jog. The coaches are always watching.

you. That's what it boils down to. You scout him like you'd scout some guy with the New Orleans Saints or something. Because if not, he's gonna beat you.

Whitfield has spent enough time around Kerney to know his teammate has a motor that he rarely turns off. It was time to learn about training camp from Kerney himself.

SOME THOUGHTS FROM PATRICK

In a March 2003 interview, Kerney, a No. 30 overall pick in 1999, finally got to enjoy a winning season for the first time in '02. The team rewarded him in midseason with a new six-year contract and an $8.5 million signing bonus.

Reporter: *Then, in some sense, I guess what you're saying is that regardless of what a coach, a teammate, a fan, or a reporter might say to you, this resolve comes from within?*

Big Whit: Here's the thing. If you're going to be successful, you say, 'I'm going to scout my man every day.' You know what I'm saying? If you're going against Brady, he's your teammate, you may not pull out all the stops. You're not going to cut-block the guy, but you know exactly what you need to do to be successful against him. You know exactly what tempo he'll be going at.

Reporter: *What about Patrick Kerney?*

Big Whit: If you're going against Patrick Kerney, you know that he will never get tired. Never get tired. So if you're going to be successful, you can never get tired. Because if you get tired, then he's going to have success against

Reporter: *Can you take me through a day at camp?*

Kerney: Get up to a loud alarm clock, 6:15 if you're hurt. Treatments are real early, 45 minutes or so. If I'm not hurt, I'll get up between 7:15 and 7:30. You've got to sign in for breakfast by 8 (a.m). Practice goes from 9 to 11 (a.m). You sit in the ice tubs after that to bring the temperature of your body down and help your legs recover. Then you shower, eat lunch, and hopefully you can squeeze in an hour nap.

Reporter: *Is the afternoon harder because the temperature is worse?*

Kerney: It depends. In the afternoon, after you get taped, you're on the field from 3 to 5. Then every other day, the receivers, quarterbacks and running backs, and the DBs lift and the next day, the (offensive and defensive) lines (and linebackers) lift. After you eat, the special teams meetings start at 7 and then position meetings start at 7:30, and they can last until 9:30 to 9:45. Then you grab a snack, usually your fourth meal of the day, and go to bed.

Continued on page 57

DICK SULLIVAN

It was like I was sitting in a meeting at Home Depot hearing Arthur say that his primary concern

At right, Dick Sullivan, newly appointed executive vice president of marketing, announces the master plan to fill the Georgia Dome on June 20, 2002.

Below, Dick sends Arthur long at the Falcons Landing kickoff. The two men were a team at Home Depot long before they teamed up with the Falcons.

*I*n nine years at The Home Depot, Dick Sullivan learned to trust his instincts and act accordingly. Arthur Blank and Bernie Marcus instilled a maverick style of management at The Home Depot that Sullivan gladly adopted. So his first meeting in the Falcons front office as executive vice president of marketing was comfortably familiar.

"It was like I was sitting in a meeting at Home Depot," Sullivan says, "hearing Arthur say that his primary concern is generating good ideas. That was the philosophy we had at Home Depot. That's our philosophy here."

Sullivan couldn't resist taking charge of the Falcons marketing team. Branding and marketing the Falcons presented real challenges, but he knew he could draw on skills and strengths he sharpened at The Home Depot—devising and implementing strategies to aggressively promote a brand that already had a public identity.

FILLING SEATS WITH HAPPY FANS

Charged with overseeing ticket sales, merchandising, radio and TV contracts, advertising, and corporate sponsorships, Sullivan comes onboard in April 2002. His first order of business is to sell thousands of empty seats. Transforming

BUILDING THE BUZZ

is generating good ideas—Dick Sullivan on his first marketing meeting at Falcons headquarters.

the game day atmosphere at the Georgia Dome is a top priority. There are some immediate issues to face. There's no place to park, much less tailgate. Traffic is snarled even when games don't sell out. There aren't enough concession stands. There's no live radio or TV feed. The screens are dim. Entertainment is limited. Is Sullivan up to the challenge the Falcons present? Arthur thinks so.

CREATE SOME BUZZ

Fortunately for Sullivan and all Falcons fans, Blank isn't concerned with receiving immediate dividends on his purchase of the team. His first priority is to strengthen the fan base and make fans love the team. Sullivan and Blank learned at The Home Depot the importance of creating a buzz in the market.

"I didn't really purchase this purely as a financial investment, per se," Blank says. "It's an investment in our community. It's an investment in our fans, for our fans—really, with our fans."

Blank has always seen the big picture and he sees it now. Even before he hires Sullivan, he meets frequently with Dome executives, Atlanta police, public transportation officials, and private owners of nearby parking lots, selling his position and making his considerable presence known. He also does what he does best. He goes to the source by conducting research with fans to hear what they want at home games. Blank wants to change the Falcons image by changing the way the team does business.

THE FALCONS THREE-POINT FAN PLAN

Blank along with his staff devise a three-point plan to attract and promote fan loyalty: **1)** Create a winning team on the field. **2)** Ensure a great game day experience. **3)** Involve every Falcons associate and player in community programs.

- Prices for 23,000 season tickets are slashed and $100 season tickets are offered in the upper-level end zones. The last time fans could attend a Falcons game for $10 was 1976, four years before Michael Vick was born.
- The team secures parking for 20,000 season ticket holders, all within a half-mile of the Dome. Only 2,000 people had spots in 2001 and each costs $160. Blank cuts that price in half.
- Police presence is increased by nearly 70 percent, and the Falcons guarantee 22 additional intersections will be patrolled.
- Food prices will not be raised, and the team says the Dome will upgrade menus.
- The Dome spends $5 million to replace the JumboTron screens with MegaVision—a video technology that's a stadium equivalent to HDTV—and to install new scoreboards and message centers.

To add value to the Falcons game day experience, Sullivan makes two important hires. One is Roddy White as director of events, marketing, and entertainment; and the other is Dave Cohen as director of ticket sales. While builds a support team and works to secure bands for shows at halftime (such as Jo Dee Messina and the Temptations) and after the game (James Brown).

BOTTOM LINE—A FULL HOUSE

"Mr. Blank isn't focused just on the bottom line. Forget that," says Jack Ragsdale, the team's longtime ticket manager. "Mr. Blank is concerned with filling the Dome with happy fans."

By the end of the 2002 season, the team has sold out all eight regular-season and two preseason games, leading to arguably the most important change of all: Blank's insistence that all games be televised in the metro Atlanta market. The NFL doesn't allow games to be shown locally if home teams don't sell all their tickets 72 hours prior to kickoff.

For all the fine-tuning, though, nothing impacts a season more than wins and losses. In the end, Michael Vick and his teammates will make the biggest difference of all.

Continued from page 53

Reporter: *Did you struggle to pace yourself earlier in your career?*

Kerney: Yeah, but everybody gets tired. It's a mental thing, and you tell yourself not to let yourself drag. You know if you need to sprint, then you better sprint. If it's OK to jog, then jog.

Reporter: *What song did the veterans make you sing your first year out of Virginia?*

Kerney: I like singing, and you can sing whatever you want. It just can't be your school song. So I did everything from John Denver to Jay-Z. They hated it when I was doing Jay-Z. That's when they told me I could stop.

Reporter: *As a rookie, how long did you need before you felt comfortable at camp, at least on the field?*

Kerney: Well, I never felt comfortable, I can tell you that. I was used to laying it all out on the field, but the thing in the NFL is adjusting to the speed of the game. You're taking three to four reps, just as much as anyone else. They're about to pass out, and so are you. That doesn't make you feel so bad when you see a veteran player getting winded.

Reporter: *Do you agree with your buddy Whitfield that off-season conditioning, passing camp, and preseason are too long?*

Kerney: Yeah, but it's a necessary evil, I guess. The length of the preseason is not for established veterans and guys they know can play. It's for guys trying to make the team or players with not much experience. It does drag on a little long, there's no doubt.

CHAPTER **THREE**   57

When the final seconds ticked off the clock in the Falcons 27-7 playoff victory over Green Bay, Patrick Kerney unchained his ego for about 10 minutes. He stood in front of the tunnel that leads to the visiting team's locker room and soaked in the snowy, surreal atmosphere.

KERR
PATRICK

Guys that work as hard as Patrick Kerney, you want to see

PATRICK **KERNEY** / Defensive end

Hard-working Patrick has started in 50 straight games since Atlanta chose him No. 30 overall out of Virginia.

58 ATLANTA FALCONS

EY

good things come their way. —Defensive line coach Bill Johnson

"You work so hard for such a long period of time that I just wanted to soak in the moment," Kerney said. "I just stood there holding my helmet, grinning from ear to ear."

Kerney, 26, had no trouble putting the moment in perspective. His first two Atlanta teams went a combined 9-23. In his third season, the Falcons were 6-4 entering December before losing four of their last five games.

Not in 2002. Atlanta went 10-7-1 and advanced to the postseason for just the seventh time in 36 years.

"Guys that work as hard as Patrick Kerney," defensive line coach Bill Johnson says, "you want to see good things come their way."

Kerney has played in every game since Atlanta chose him No. 30 overall out of Virginia. He has started 50 straight games, none of which could match the satisfaction he felt after the Falcons playoff win over Green Bay.

He pulled Travis Hall aside and made the massive defensive tackle stand with him.

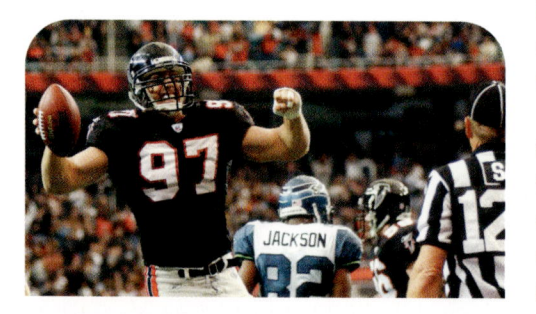

No. 97 throws himself headfirst into every game. He's a playbreaker with lots of reason to celebrate and lots of years left in the NFL.

Patrick's determination and intensity are evident in his eyes. He's a perfect example of hard work and dedication paying off in spades.

2002 INDIVIDUAL STATS / Patrick Kerney

Sacks	10.5
Tackles	104
Fumbles recovered	2
Touchdowns	1
Height	6'5"
Weight	273

97

"You've got to stop for a minute and soak this in," Kerney told Hall. "We've been through too much to just walk in there and not enjoy this for a minute."

ATLANTA FALCONS

If you're going against Patrick Kerney, you know he'll never get tired. Never get tired. So if you're going to be successful, you can never get tired. —Bob Whitfield

CHAPTER FOUR

THE PRE

Veterans like punter Chris Mohr (13), right, and defensive end Brady Smith (91), top, use the preseason to work on technique and timing. Mohr, a 14-year pro, and Smith, an eight-year vet, have no concern about job security. The Falcons put together a perfect record in four preseason games.

SEASON

Preseason in the NFL is a laboratory for the coaches. Game plans are tested. Rookies are given chances to shine. It's all about finding rhythm offensively, pulling the defense together, and building a team to compete in the regular season.

For guys like Keith Lyle, left, a one-time star of the St. Louis secondary, preseason is all about winning a job and staying in the NFL another year. Lyle, though, will receive a pink slip before the regular season begins.

*T*he preseason stars are many—T.J. Duckett, Doug Johnson, Jay Feely, the offensive line, and Michael Vick too. In the four-game exhibition season, they each have moments in the spotlight as the Falcons post victories over Jacksonville, New York, Dallas, and Cincinnati. Of those teams, only the Giants will prove to be playoff-caliber, but that doesn't matter as Dan Reeves' team, trying to build on the previous season's 7-9 record, discovers who will make the big plays and gains confidence with each victory.

CHAPTER **FOUR**

8.09.2002   FALCONS vs. *JACKSONVILLE JAGUARS* > > > Played at Atlanta > >

FIRST PRESEASON GAME

FOR THE FIRST TIME SINCE THE BUILDING OPENED IN 1992, THE GEORGIA DOME IS PACKED FOR A PRESEASON GAME. BLANK & CO. HAVE APPROXIMATELY 52,000 IN THE HOUSE AND SELL ENOUGH TICKETS TO GET THE LOCAL TELEVISION BLACKOUT LIFTED.

NICE SHINE
Those old, grainy Jumbotron screens that hung over the club-level seats in the end zones have been replaced by crystal-clear Megavision boards that Dome officials claim can run 50 years without a noticeable loss of brightness.

INJURY UPDATE
Rookie Will Overstreet, hurt at training camp three days earlier, doesn't play. An MRI shows a partial tear of cartilage in his right shoulder. Expected to start at outside linebacker, Overstreet is scheduled to see James Andrews, a renowned orthopedist in Birmingham, Ala.

HOLD THAT BALL
Two lost fumbles lead to Jacksonville field goals in the second quarter. Though Bob Christian is the first Falcon to lose control of the football, he is a starting fullback and a 10-year veteran in no danger of losing his job. Travis McGriff, on the other hand, is a free agent battling for the fifth and final job as a receiver. A former standout receiver at Florida and a third-round draft pick for Denver in 1999, McGriff fumbles away a punt return at his own 20-yard line. He will be among the final group of cuts on Aug. 31.

HOLD THAT TONGUE
Doug Johnson silences the calls for a veteran backup quarterback by playing the entire second half and completing 14 of 15 passes for 151 yards. He directs an 88-yard, 12-play scoring drive early in the third quarter, the biggest gainer covering 27 yards on a pass over the middle to tight end Reggie Kelly; and a 10-play, 83-yard drive ending the final two minutes with Travis Jervey's 1-yard touchdown run.

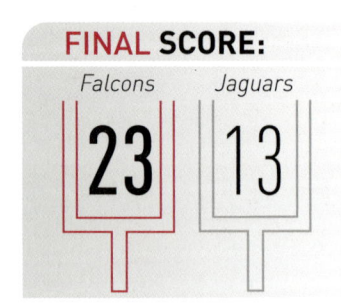

FINAL SCORE:
Falcons 23 — Jaguars 13

First-round draft pick T.J. Duckett, bottom, wants to make a good first impression in his first NFL game. The same goes for No. 2 quarterback Doug Johnson, below, a two-year veteran who will remove doubts that he can handle the responsibility of backing up Michael Vick. Marques McFadden, though, is less fortunate. A street free agent with no experience, McFadden, No. 67, will be among the final wave of cuts on Aug. 31.

THE GAME STILL BOILS DOWN TO TURNOVERS, AND I THOUGHT THOSE TWO TURNOVERS REALLY HURT US OFFENSIVELY IN THE FIRST HALF. BUT THE DEFENSIVE GUYS ARE FLYING TO THE FOOTBALL. I'M REALLY PLEASED WITH THAT. —DAN REEVES

Doug Johnson is sensational in his 2002 preseason debut, playing the entire second half and completing 14 of 15 passes for 151 yards.

DUCKETT DELIVERS

First-round draft pick T.J. Duckett carries six times for 35 yards on the first touchdown drive in the third quarter. The former Michigan State star missed the first nine days of training camp in a holdout for a bigger contract, but he erases concerns after breaking off a 25-yard run.

CHAPTER **FOUR** 65

8.17.2002   FALCONS vs. *N.Y. GIANTS* > > > Played at Atlanta > > >

SECOND PRESEASON GAME

AN ANNOUNCED CROWD OF 67,204, THE LARGEST PRESEASON GATE IN FRANCHISE HISTORY, WATCHES JAY FEELY KICK FIVE FIELD GOALS AND NEW YORK LOSE SIX TURNOVERS. AN UNMISTAKABLE AIR OF OPTIMISM ENVELOPES AN ATLANTA TEAM WITH JUST THREE WINNING RECORDS IN THE PAST 18 YEARS.

JUST WARMING UP
Michael Vick throws his first touchdown pass of the preseason, a 2-yard strike to tight end Alge Crumpler to put the Falcons ahead 10-7.

BETTER WATCH OUT
Defensive ends Patrick Kerney and Brady Smith take turns sacking New York quarterback Kerry Collins and forcing fumbles. Linebacker Matt Stewart recovers both loose balls.

DOMINANT NIGHT
The Giants look unstoppable on their opening drive, a nine-play, 77-yard effort that ends with Collins' 1-yard touchdown pass to sensational rookie tight end Jeremy Shockey, but Atlanta's defense ends the night having allowed only 73 net yards rushing and 177 passing.

QUOTE OF THE DAY
New York defensive end Michael Strahan, who set an NFL single-season record with 22.5 sacks in 2001, feels helpless on the Falcons second drive. Strahan crushes running back Warrick Dunn in the backfield, only to find that Vick is clutching the ball and beginning a 19-yard run.

"Hey, you guys see what I see," Strahan says. "He's elusive and he has a great arm—and that's on film. In person, wow. He has all the intangibles. It's just a matter of him growing into his role. He will be a quarterback in this league for a long time, and a very impressive one at that."

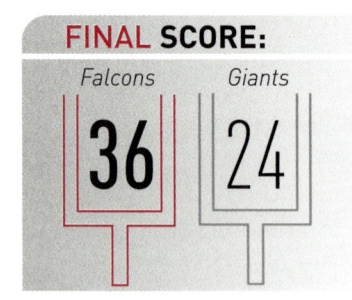

FINAL SCORE:
Falcons 36   Giants 24

The Falcons spread the ball around—and have a lot of points to show for it—in their second preseason game.

Warrick Dunn (28) leads the Falcons with seven rushes. He also catches two passes as Atlanta puts three touchdowns and five field goals on the Georgia Dome scoreboard.

66   ATLANTA FALCONS

THE DEFENSE DID A GREAT JOB CREATING TURNOVERS. WE PUT SOME POINTS ON THE BOARD AND THAT'S THE MOST IMPORTANT THING. —MICHAEL VICK

The Falcons offensive line holds Michael Strahan without a sack while opening holes that lead to 124 yards on the ground.

CHAPTER **FOUR** 67

8.24.2002   FALCONS vs. DALLAS COWBOYS > > > Played at Dallas > > >

THIRD PRESEASON GAME

A SCARE SHOOTS THROUGH THE ENTIRE ORGANIZATION WHEN DALLAS DEFENSIVE ENDS LA'ROI GLOVER AND EBENEZER EKUBAN APPLY A SECOND-QUARTER SANDWICH SACK TO MICHAEL VICK THAT FORCES THE QUARTERBACK TO BE ESCORTED OFF THE FIELD, HIS RIGHT ELBOW HEAVILY WRAPPED IN ICE.

JUST RELAX
Vick, a left-hander, has suffered only a bruise and should be ready for the season opener in two weeks at Green Bay.

ROLL CALL
Right tackle Todd Weiner, the man responsible for protecting Vick's blind side, remains in Atlanta with a bruised left shoulder. Backup fullback George Layne also stays behind after suffering a concussion against the Giants.

GOOD MOVES
Doug Johnson completes 14 of 21 passes for 195 yards and two touchdowns. He hits Willie Jackson on a fly pattern down the left seam, a beautifully scripted 18-yarder that the receiver catches over his right shoulder in the end zone to beat cornerback Jason Bell for a 7-3 Atlanta lead in the final minute of the second quarter. Early in the fourth, Johnson throws a 41-yard bomb that a wide-open Alvis Whitted catches at the 5 and runs in for a 14-13 lead. Third-string QB Kurt Kittner, a rookie from Illinois, connects with tight end Brian Kozlowski on a 30-yard touchdown to make it 21-13.

BAD MOVES
Johnson, who throws two interceptions, is trying to find receiver Brian Finneran early in the third when right guard Kynan Forney pulls left on what looks to be a busted play. Safety Tony Dixon stunts from the middle of the line and hammers the Atlanta QB, whose pass is picked off by linebacker Marcus Steele, who returns it 34 yards for a 13-7 Dallas lead.

FINAL SCORE:
Falcons 21   Cowboys 19

Despite Michael Vick taking just 14 snaps before leaving the game with an injury, the Falcons improve their preseason record to 3-0.

Tight ends Brian Kozlowski (85) and Alge Crumpler lead Atlanta with four receptions apiece. Kozlowski's big catch comes on a 30-yard scoring pass in the fourth quarter that gives the Falcons their winning points.

ATLANTA FALCONS

Even after his elbow is banged up, Vick shows the kind of stubborn resolve a team needs from a starting quarterback. "I just got hit and I lost the feeling for a little bit. The X-rays are negative. It won't set me back, but still I wanted to get as many reps as possible." —Michael Vick

Atlanta's defense gives up 135 yards on the ground, but the NFL's all-time leading rusher, Emmitt Smith, gains just 25 yards.

CHAPTER **FOUR** 69

8.29.2002 FALCONS vs. *CINCINNATI BENGALS* > > > Played at Cincinnati > >

FOURTH PRESEASON GAME

MICHAEL VICK SHOWS NO ILL EFFECTS FROM THE PREVIOUS WEEK, AND WARRICK DUNN AND T.J. DUCKETT PROVIDE A GLIMPSE OF A HOPEFUL FUTURE WITH BREAKOUT PERFORMANCES IN THE BACKFIELD. BAD NEWS STRIKES IN THE FINAL THREE MINUTES WHEN WILL OVERSTREET LIES MOTIONLESS ON THE FIELD AFTER DISLOCATING HIS TENDER SHOULDER.

FINAL SCORE:
Falcons 27 Bengals 14

PRACTICE MAKES PERFECT
Atlanta finishes the preseason 4-0. The last time the Falcons went unbeaten in exhibition play was 1990, a season that ended with a 5-11 record in Jerry Glanville's first year as head coach.

GOOD OMEN 1
Though he enters with only three preseason receptions for 14 yards, Dunn steals the spotlight on the second drive, catching a pass over the middle from Vick and scampering 36 yards to the Cincinnati 30. Four plays later, at the start of the second quarter, Dunn lays a vicious block on blitzing defensive end Justin Smith, giving Vick enough time to hit Shawn Jefferson for a 12-yard completion to the 3. On the next play, Dunn takes a handoff and outruns safety Cory Hall for his first Atlanta touchdown.

RUMBLING:
Duckett has two modest runs before running through the Bengals for a 24-yard touchdown and a 14-7 lead the Falcons don't relinquish.

STRONG FINISH
Matt Stewart ends a strong preseason by sacking Gus Frerotte for a 5-yard loss on the Bengals first drive and sacking him for a 9-yard loss on their second.

GOOD OMEN 2
Starting receiver Brian Finneran plays defense on the final play of the second quarter. Placed in the end zone as Jon Kitna attempts a long bomb, the 6-foot-5 Finneran steps up and makes the interception.

With 21 unanswered points in the second quarter, Atlanta wraps up an undefeated preseason, winning twice at home and twice on the road.

Patrick Kerney (97) and the Falcons defense make their presence known early, sacking Cincinnati quarterback Gus Ferotte twice in the first quarter. The defense also comes up with five turnovers in the victory.

70 ATLANTA FALCONS

Preseason showed us we've got the talent to get the job done. We wanted to try to get better over the four games and I believe we did. Unfortunately we start the regular season 0-0 just like everybody else. —Dan Reeves

Third-round draft pick Will Overstreet (90), right, forces a fumble, then leaves the field with a dislocated left shoulder.

CHAPTER **FOUR** 71

2002 SEASON HIGHLIGHTS

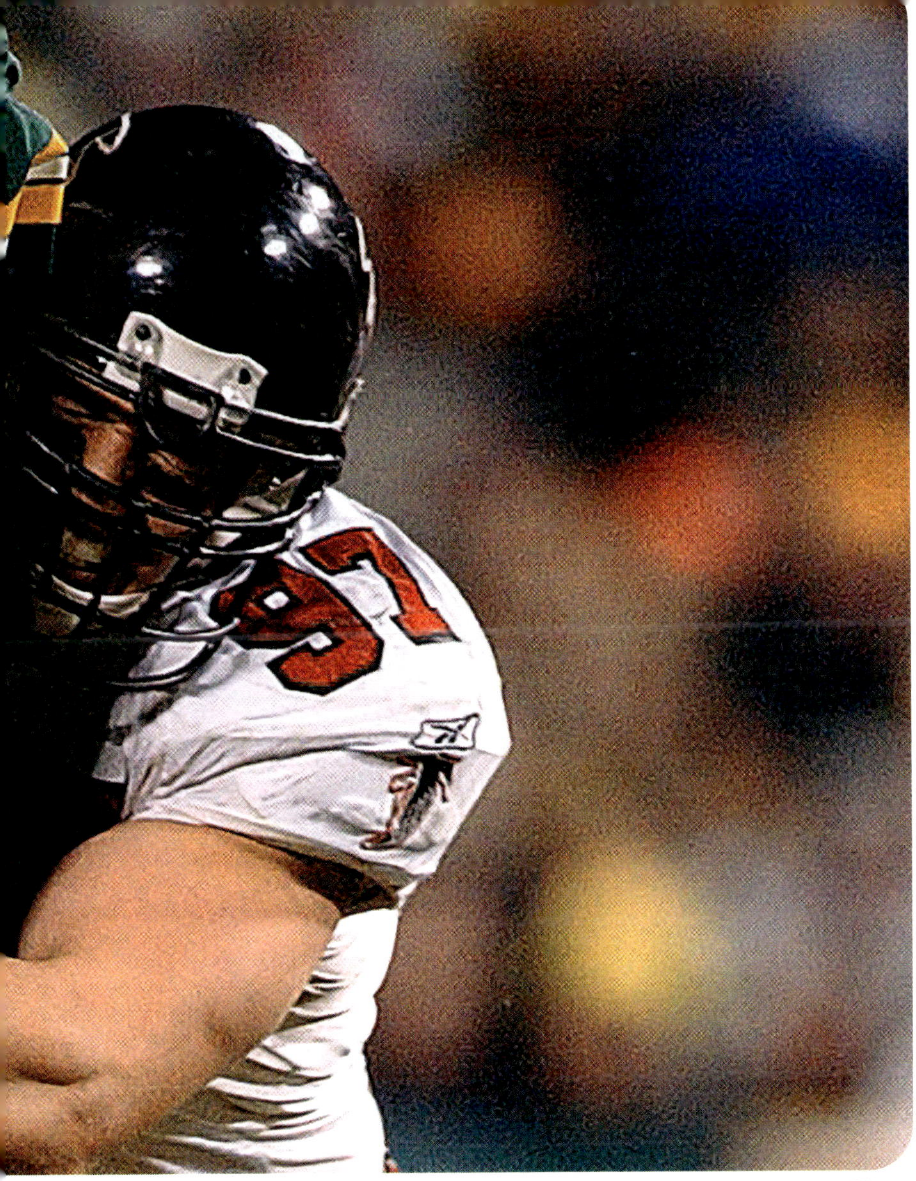

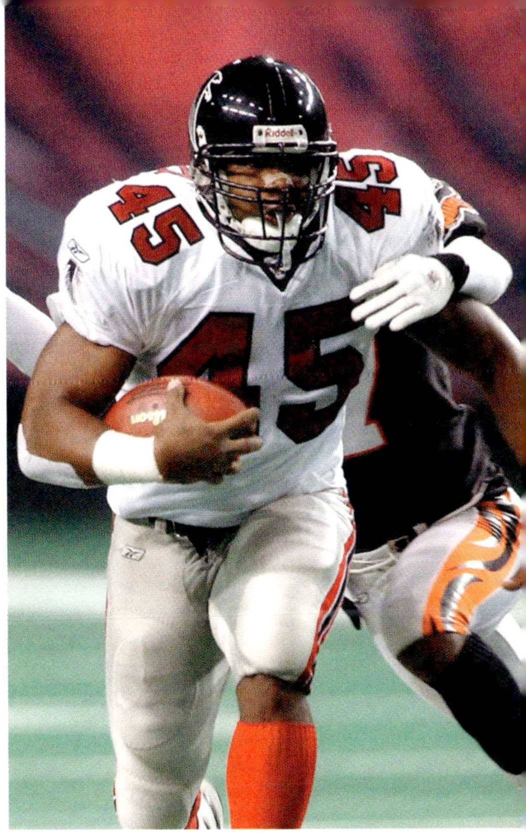

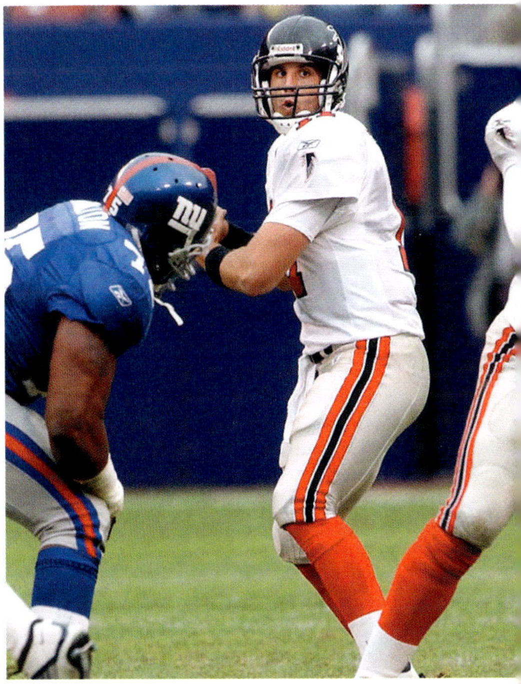

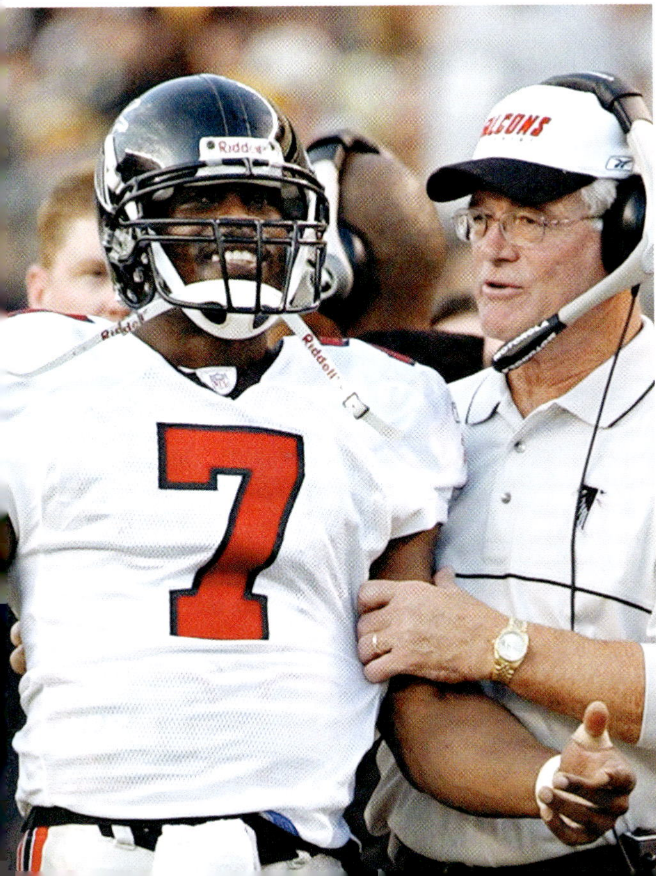
Telex

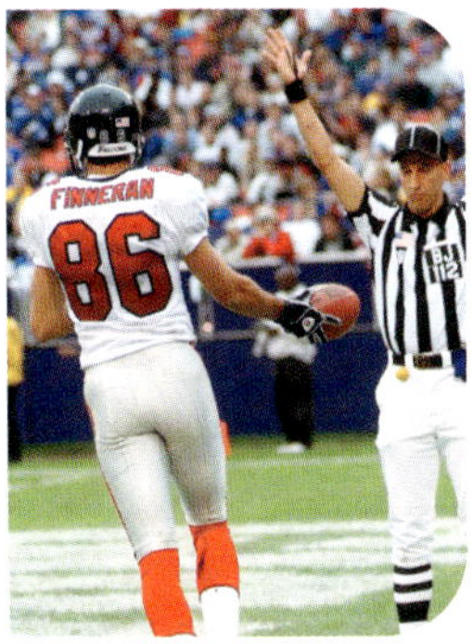

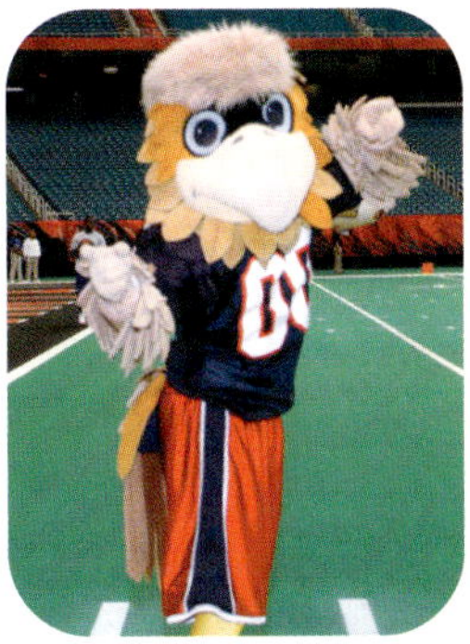

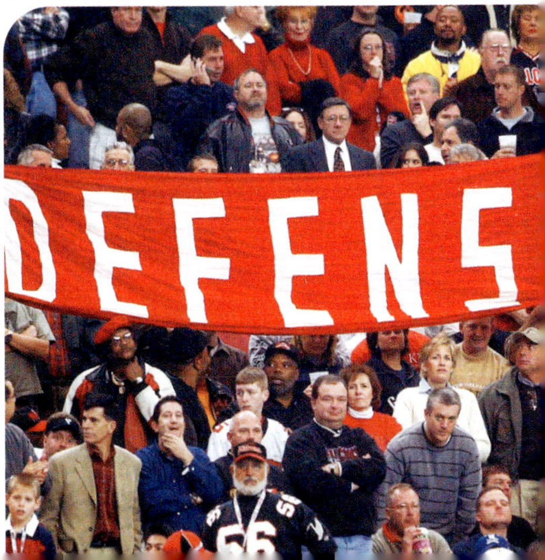
DEFENS

CHAPTER FIVE
BEEN THERE, DONE

2002 REGULAR SEASON—GAMES 1-4

9.08.2002   FALCONS vs. *GREEN BAY PACKERS*

PLAYING THE PACK

WE HAVE A LOT OF CHARACTER. THAT'S THE BIGGEST DIFFERENCE.
—BOB CHRISTIAN

GREEN BAY. The Falcons enter Lambeau Field wondering how Michael Vick will handle the pressure of starting. But he rises to the occasion on a broiling afternoon with 10 consecutive completions at the start of the game showing the kind of composure that's made Green Bay's Brett Favre a legend.

The game escapes Atlanta in overtime partly due to an injury-wrought defensive front that allows Ahman Green 155 yards rushing, Favre's usual savvy, and some questionable officiating on a late Green Bay drive when the Falcons felt they had stopped the Packers short of the end zone.

Vick finishes 15-for-23 passing for 209 yards and a 2-yard touchdown pass to tight end Alge Crumpler at the end of the second quarter. Jay Feely's 52-yard field goal pushes the game into overtime but Green Bay wins the 3½-hour spectacle with a 34-yard field goal into the wind.

"They played great," Favre says after the game. "The difference this year was that we made some crucial plays."

"We have a lot of character—that's the biggest difference," fullback Bob Christian says. "We're a little banged up, but we're pulling together."

"We did what we had to do," Feely says. "We played a great game. It's just a shame that they got guys out there who should be wearing cheeseheads instead of white caps. I mean give me a break."

Kerney makes seven tackles and gets one of the Falcons two sacks against the Packers.

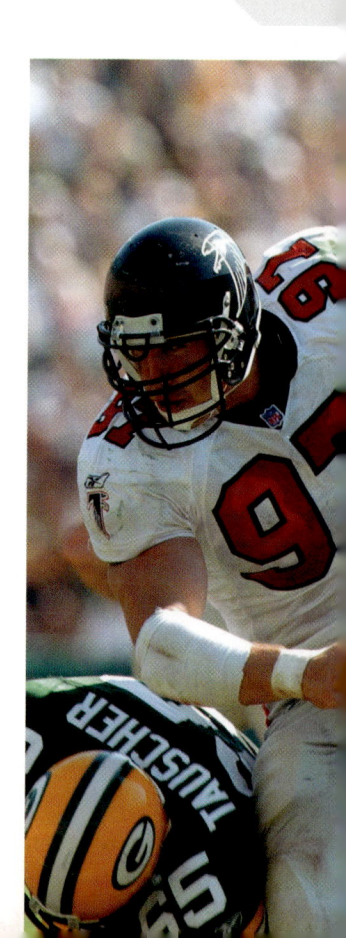

ATLANTA FALCONS

THAT

The Falcons stop Donald Driver short of the end zone on this play, but Green Bay scores seven of the 12 times it has the ball in the overtime victory at Lambeau Field.

Played at Green Bay > > > Attendance: 63,127 > > >

INDIVIDUAL LEADERS
RUSHING > Atlanta: *Vick 9-72 1 td* > Green Bay: *Green 27-155*
PASSING > Atlanta: *Vick 15-23-209 1 td* > Green Bay: *Favre 25-36-284 2 tds*
RECEIVING > Atlanta: *Jackson 4-73* > Green Bay: *Driver 7-78*

FINAL SCORE: (OT)

Packers **37** — Falcons **34**

Atlanta	0	21	3	10	0	**34**
Green Bay	3	10	14	7	3	**37**

1st Quarter
GB–Longwell 28 FG

2nd Quarter
Atl–Vick 2 run (Feely kick)
Atl–Dunn 3 run (Feely kick)
GB–Martin 3 pass from Favre (Longwell kick)
Atl–Crumpler 2 pass from Vick (Feely kick)
GB–Longwell 42 FG

3rd Quarter
GB–Mealey 2 run (Longwell kick)
Atl–Feely 21 FG
GB–Walker 13 pass from Favre (Longwell kick)

4th Quarter
Atl–Dunn 2 run (Feely kick)
GB–Henderson 1 run (Longwell kick)
Atl–Feely 52 FG

Overtime
GB–Longwell 34 FG

TEAM STATS 9/08/02

	Atl	GB
First Downs	22	29
Total Net Yards	374	484
Rushes-Yards	30-180	38-211
Passing Yards	194	273
Passes Comp-Att-Int	15-23-0	25-36-0
Sacked-Yards	4-15	2-11
Penalties-Yards	4-82	3-15
Fumbles-Lost	2-1	3-1
Time of Possession	30:55	38:50

9.15.2002   FALCONS vs. CHICAGO BEARS

PLAYING THE BEARS

WE CAME AWAY FROM THE RED ZONE TOO MANY TIMES WITH NOTHING OR THREE POINTS. THOSE ALWAYS COME BACK TO HAUNT YOU. —DAN REEVES

ATLANTA. Say what you want about Jay Feely's two missed field goals, the second a 45-yard attempt that sails left of the uprights and guarantees a 14-13 loss to the Chicago Bears and disappointment for the 68,081 who nearly fill the Georgia Dome.

The Falcons drop to 0-2 in this still-promising season because of three lost fumbles in a 3:48 span early in the third quarter.

Though Chicago commits a turnover during that stretch and scores only when Jim Miller hits David Terrell for a 14-yard touchdown and a 14-10 lead, Atlanta's offense has several misfires that seal the game.

"We came away from the red zone too many times with nothing or three points," says coach Dan Reeves, whose team gains 78 yards on 27 plays in the second half. "Those always come back to haunt you."

Indeed. A 67-yard kickoff return from Travis Jervey gives the Falcons great field position at the 23, but after reaching first-and-goal at the 9, they

The Falcons hold Chicago's Dez White to one catch but have trouble generating offense of their own.

FINAL SCORE:

Bears **14**   Falcons **13**

Atlanta	0	10	3	0	**13**
Chicago	0	7	7	0	**14**

2nd Quarter
Atl–Dunn 10 pass from Vick (Feely kick)
Chi–Thomas 3 run (Edinger kick)
Atl–Feely 37 FG

3rd Quarter
Chi–Terrell 14 pass from Miller (Edinger kick)
Atl–Feely 27 FG

76   ATLANTA FALCONS

Played at Atlanta > > > Attendance: 68,081 > > >

INDIVIDUAL LEADERS RUSHING > Atlanta: *Vick 10-56* > Chicago: *Thomas 26-84-1 td*
PASSING > Atlanta: *Vick 17-28-166 1 td* > Chicago: *Miller 12-24-143 1 td, 1 int.*
RECEIVING > Atlanta: *Finneran 6-76* > Chicago: *Booker 5-48*

Michael Vick provides most of Atlanta's offense against the Bears, running for 56 yards and passing for 166. But the Falcons reach the end zone just once as five drives end with punts and the team loses two fumbles and misses two field goals.

advance no farther and have to settle for Feely's 27-yard field goal to end the scoring.

THINK ABOUT THE BIG PICTURE

What does an 0-2 start mean to the Falcons? Not much if you consider that New England had the same record last year before winning its first Super Bowl.

"Well, it's a long season," Warrick Dunn says. "I don't think guys are like, 'Let's give up on the season after two games.' We're going to get back and look at it and we'll challenge each other. Guys have to get up and make plays."

TEAM STATS 9.15.2002

	Chi	Atl
First Downs	13	19
Total Net Yards	242	257
Rushes-Yards	31-106	30-122
Passing Yards	136	135
Passes Comp-Att-Int	12-24-1	17-28-0
Sacked-Yards	1-7	4-31
Penalties-Yards	7-79	5-40
Fumbles-Lost	2-1	3-3
Time of Possession	28:35	31:25

CHAPTER FIVE

WH BOB

Whitfield comes to play every game no matter how he feels. "It seems like closer to game day you

...don't feel the pain as much. For the most part I've just been lucky, I guess."

No player in franchise history has started more consecutive games than Bob Whitfield, but asking Whitfield to explain his longevity is like finding an unlabeled tape and pressing "play" on the cassette deck: Prepare to be surprised.

On this occasion, the 6-foot-5, 310-pound Whitfield credits tiny Mr. Miyagi, "The Karate Kid" character Pat Morita made famous in the 1984 feature film, with being a source of strength.

Week in and week out for 11 NFL seasons, offensive tackle Bob Whitfield proves himself to be one of the most durable Falcons in franchise history.

BOB **WHITFIELD** — Offensive Lineman

An eighth-round draft pick, Whitfield was an all-American tackle at Stanford under coach Dennis Green, then immediately stepped into a starting role with the Falcons.

CHAPTER **FIVE**   79

"Ancient Chinese secret—Old Mr. Miyagi's secret," Whitfield says. "But I better knock on wood now because you done cursed me and (stuff). I just go out and play. You know what I'm saying? Mind over matter. It just don't hurt."

Whitfield, a Stanford man who's made several million dollars playing football and owning an Atlanta recording studio, loves to talk trash. He always has a good comeback line. The subject of injuries, though, is cut short. An 11-year veteran, particularly one who's healthy, doesn't want to jinx himself.

Since the Falcons drafted him No. 8 overall in 1992 and he won a job the following year, Whitfield has started all but one of the Falcons 165 games.

Whitfield's franchise-record streak of 123 consecutive starts ended in 2000 with a jammed neck, but his durability

He's a Pro Bowler—tackle Bob Whitfield was first selected to play in the NFL all-star game in 1998.

ALL-PRO — Bob Whitfield

Most consecutive games started for the Falcons

1. Bob Whitfield	1993-2000	123
2. Jeff Van Note	1970-1984	112
3. Steve Bartkowski	1977-1984	100
4. Terance Mathis	1996-2001	96
5. Mike Kenn	1978-1984	90
6. Jessie Tuggle	1992-1997	89

70

He's all-Madden too—Whitfield was selected to TV commentator John Madden's all-star team in 1995 and 2001.

has never been questioned.

"You know what you can tolerate and what you can't," Whitfield says. "I think, you know, what I had I've always been able to tolerate. It seems like closer to game day, you don't feel the pain as much. For the most part I've just been lucky, I guess."

Whitfield's franchise-record streak of 123 consecutive starts ended in 2000 with a jammed neck, but his durability has never been questioned.

CHAPTER **FIVE** 81

9.22.2002 FALCONS vs. CINCINNATI BENGALS

PLAYING THE BENGALS

THE FALCONS CAGE THE BENGALS FOR THE FIRST WIN OF THE SEASON AND ARTHUR BLANK GETS THE GAME BALL FROM DAN REEVES.

ATLANTA. Michael Vick makes sure the Falcons keep pace in the NFC South.

The 22-year-old quarterback does it all in a Sunday night game, completing 16 of 26 passes for 174 yards and two touchdowns to Brian Finneran as the Falcons beat the Cincinnati Bengals, 30-3.

Entering an off-week, Atlanta (1-2) needs a win after New Orleans and Carolina improve to 3-0; and the Falcons next opponent, Tampa Bay, has a 2-1 start.

"We could easily be 3-0, but that's the way the game goes," Vick says. "Hopefully, this is a stepping stone for our team, and we can win the next 13 games. That's our goal."

ARTHUR GETS THE BALL

Though Vick is nearly unstoppable, head coach Dan Reeves gives new owner Arthur Blank the game ball.

Wide receiver Brian Finneran (86) gets into the end zone twice as the Bengals dare the Falcons to beat them through the air.

82 ATLANTA FALCONS

Played at Atlanta > > > Attendance: 68,129 > > >

INDIVIDUAL LEADERS RUSHING > Atlanta: *Duckett 18-67* > Cincinnati: *Dillon 18-66*
PASSING > Atlanta: *Vick 26-16-174 2 tds* > Cincinnati: *Kitna 35-18-136 1 int.*
RECEIVING > Atlanta: *Finneran 6-77 2 tds* > Cincinnati: *Warrick 4-34*

FINAL SCORE:

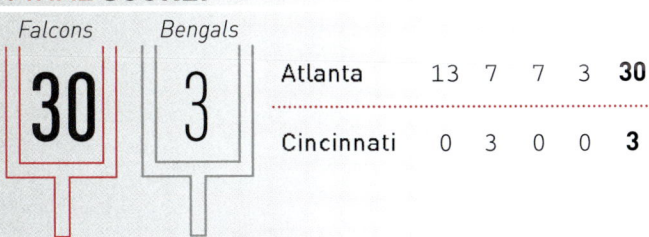

Falcons **30** — Bengals **3**

Atlanta	13	7	7	3	**30**
Cincinnati	0	3	0	0	**3**

1st Quarter
Atl–Feely 44 FG
Atl–Feely 26 FG
Atl–Finneran 20 pass from Vick (Feely kick)

2nd Quarter
Atl–Finneran 13 pass from Vick (Feely kick)
Cin–Rackers 24 FG

3rd Quarter
Atl–Dunn 4 run (Feely kick)

4th Quarter
Atl–Feely 34 FG

Vick leads the Atlanta resurgence, and the Falcons beat Cincinnati to avoid falling into a hole in the NFC South.

"We'd been trying to give him one the first two weeks, but we couldn't get the job done," Reeves says. "They're pretty excited in (the locker room). The guys have been awfully close the last couple of weeks."

Vick is sensational in his first nationally televised game, running five times for 56 yards and seemingly gaining yards at will.

"I was playing under control," he says. "I felt I could basically take over the game."

"I thought Mike made a lot of outstanding plays just like he did the first two games," Reeves says. "They were almost daring us to throw the football with the way they were stuffing the run in the first half."

TEAM STATS 9.22.2002

	Cin	Atl
First Downs	11	18
Total Net Yards	193	306
Rushes-Yards	20-68	36-143
Passing Yards	125	163
Passes Comp-Att-Int	18-42-2	16-26-0
Sacked-Yards	2-11	1-11
Penalties-Yards	8-72	7-70
Fumbles-Lost	1-0	0-0
Time of Possession	23:15	36:45

CHAPTER **FIVE** 83

10.6.2002 FALCONS vs. TAMPA BAY BUCCANEERS

PLAYING THE BUCS

A DEFENSIVE FRONT THAT GOOD—YOU'RE NOT GOING TO HOLD 'EM DOWN. THEY'RE GOING TO GET IN THERE AND KNOCK YOU AROUND A LITTLE BIT. —MICHAEL VICK

ATLANTA. The artificial turf is wet enough to make Michael Vick change his shoes at halftime, but the playing surface at the Georgia Dome hasn't softened up any.

No amount of extra padding can save Vick from Tampa Bay's relentless defense. The Buccaneers spend the first half robbing Vick of his swagger. By Atlanta's third play of the third quarter, they send him to the sideline for good.

"Once he's out of the game, it's lights out," Bucs defensive tackle Warren Sapp says.

Because he fears losing a fumble as he runs to his right, Vick holds the ball tightly against his body with both hands as Simeon Rice makes a diving sack for a 6-yard loss at the Falcons 28. Vick has no alternative but to let his right shoulder absorb the brunt of his body weight crashing to the turf.

T.J. Duckett (45) has 11 rushes and gains 52 of the Falcons 70 rushing yards.

The look of determination on the face of defensive end Brady Smith (91) at the end of a tough game says that the Bucs haven't seen the last of this Falcons team.

TEAM STATS 10.06.2002

	TB	Atl
First Downs	15	14
Total Net Yards	327	243
Rushes-Yards	26-74	22-70
Passing Yards	253	173
Passes Comp-Att-Int	17-31-1	17-38-4
Sacked-Yards	2-8	4-14
Penalties-Yards	6-35	6-41
Fumbles-Lost	1-1	0-0
Time of Possession	29:34	30:26

Played at Atlanta > > > Attendance: 68,936 > > >

INDIVIDUAL LEADERS RUSHING > Atlanta: *Duckett 11-52* > Tampa Bay: *Pittman 19-62*
PASSING > Atlanta: *D. Johnson 13-25-150 3 int.* > Tampa Bay: *B. Johnson 17-31-261 1 td 1 int.*
RECEIVING > Atlanta: *Finneran 5-61* > Tampa Bay: *K. Johnson 6-131 1 td*

FINAL SCORE:

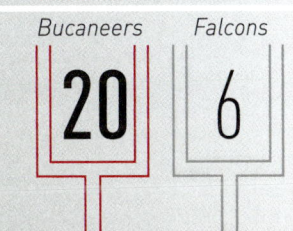

Bucaneers **20** Falcons **6**

Atlanta	3	0	3	0	**6**
Tampa Bay	0	3	7	10	**20**

1st Quarter
Atl–Feely 34 FG
2nd Quarter
TB–Gramatica 23 FG
3rd Quarter
Atl–Feely 32 FG
TB–K. Johnson 76 pass from B. Johnson (Gramatica kick)
4th Quarter
TB–Gramatica 22 FG
TB–Brooks 15 int. return (Gramatica kick)

"A defensive front that good—you're not going to hold 'em down," says Vick, whose head bounces hard off the turf. "They're going to get in there and knock you around a little bit."

Vick walks away from the Dome with a shred of good news. X-rays taken on his right nonthrowing shoulder are negative, and the Falcons franchise cornerstone might be ready when Atlanta travels to New York next week to pace the Giants.

"We would do some things well and then stop ourselves and let them stop us. They are a great defensive team and they are great at what they do," coach Dan Reeves says of the Bucs.

Michael Vick struggles early against the Buccaneers defense.

CHAPTER **FIVE**

CHAPTER SIX
GIANT KILLERS
2002 REGULAR SEASON—GAMES 5-8

10.13.2002   FALCONS vs. *NY GIANTS*

PLAYING THE GIANTS

DOUG JOHNSON DOES MORE THAN FILL IN FOR INJURED STARTER MICHAEL VICK. BY BEATING THE GIANTS, HE KEEPS THE FALCONS IN THE HUNT.

NEW JERSEY. Just as the Falcons are in danger of having their season buried in the swampy Meadowlands around Giants Stadium, quarterback Doug Johnson refuses to buckle. The third-year backup quarterback, in his first start since December 2000, makes the plays necessary to keep Atlanta's hopes alive.

Johnson does more than fill in for injured starter Michael Vick. He also prevents the Falcons, who improve to 2-3, from losing on the same day Tampa Bay and New Orleans go to 5-1.

DAMAGE CONTROL
Johnson completes 19 of 25 passes and helps produce both touchdowns. His 257 yards passing are a single-game season high for Atlanta. He handles the adversity of fumbling on each of his two sacks, one that running back T.J. Duckett recovers at the Atlanta 13 in the first quarter and another that Johnson himself recovers on the first drive of the third quarter.

THINK LIKE A PRO
The former Florida standout also runs
Continued on page 89

No. 2 quarterback Doug Johnson passes for 257 yards and gets a fourth-quarter touchdown to keep the Falcons winning while Michael Vick is on the mend.

86   ATLANTA **FALCONS**

In a pressure-cooker atmosphere, the Falcons defensive line keeps the pressure on the Giants. New York had the ball for 19:01 in the second half, compared to 11:09 for Atlanta.

Played at New Jersey > > > Attendance: 78,728 > > >

INDIVIDUAL LEADERS RUSHING > Atlanta: *Duckett 16-36* > New York: *Barber 14-57*
PASSING > Atlanta: *Johnson 19-25-257 1 td* > New York: *Collins 20-31-207 1 td, 1 int.*
RECEIVING > Atlanta: *Dunn 7-69* > New York: *Hilliard 7-76-1 td*

FINAL SCORE:

Falcons **17**   *Giants* **10**

Atlanta	0	10	0	7	**17**
New York	0	3	7	0	**10**

2nd Quarter
Atl–Johnson 15 run (Feely kick)
NY–Bryant 38 FG
Atl–Feely 31 FG

3rd Quarter
NY–Hilliard 18 pass from Collins (Bryant kick)

4th Quarter
Atl–Finneran 14 pass from Johnson (Feely kick)

TEAM STATS 10.13.2002

	Atl	NY
First Downs	15	18
Total Net Yards	313	306
Rushes-Yards	24-67	27-113
Passing Yards	246	193
Passes Comp-Att-Int	19-25-0	20-31-1
Sacked-Yards	2-11	3-14
Penalties-Yards	3-20	6-35
Fumbles-Lost	2-0	3-1
Time of Possession	29:58	30:02

DOUG JOHNSON

Doug Johnson's quarterbacking skills were put to the test in the Meadowlands. He rose to the occasion and was a major force in starting the Falcons eight-game winning streak.

Doug Johnson is comfortable as a backup to Michael Vick. It suits him well—for now, at least. He's familiar with the role, having played for Steve Spurrier at Florida. Spending four years on Florida's quarterback carousel prepared Johnson for his first three years in the league behind Chris Chandler in 2000 and behind Chandler and Vick in '01.

Any player who lasts several seasons in the NFL has strong skills, but Johnson's job requires the right kind of humility too. He's smart enough to understand how a former undrafted college free agent compares to a No. 1 overall draft pick.

"Everybody knows this is Mike's team," Johnson says. "That's just the way it is. In order for me to be a starter, everybody knows I have to go somewhere else. Until that time presents itself, I'd love to stay here as long as I have to because I think the organization is first-class. I'm in a great situation right now."

DOUG JOHNSON / Quarterback

Acquired as a free agent in 2000, Johnson makes for a strong-armed back-up to Michael Vick. He started 22 games for Florida between 1996 and 1999.

88 ATLANTA FALCONS

Continued from page 86

for his first NFL touchdown when he fakes out Jason Sehorn, New York's celebrated cornerback, for a 15-yard touchdown run that gives the Falcons a 7-0 lead early in the second quarter.

Johnson's game management is impressive, and Atlanta's defense shines as well.

DEFENSIVE DOMINANCE

Johnson and Brian Finneran are able to connect on the game's final score thanks in part to cornerback Juran Bolden intercepting Kerry Collins at the Atlanta 6 early in the fourth. Later in the locker room, Bolden still can't remember stepping in front of Ike Hilliard over the middle. "Actually, I forgot I caught the ball because somebody came and said they coldcocked me, and my whole head hit the ground," Bolden says.

QUOTE OF THE DAY

"I remember Doug coming in the huddle and saying, 'Look, I need good protection on this,' and I remember him telling T.J., 'I need a great fake on this.' I just had to get by that guy. It just worked out. Doug hung it up there, and I went and got it," Shawn Jefferson says of his 63-yard catch on a play-action fake that follows Bolden's interception.

One play turns the tide in the Meadowlands. Cornerback Juran Bolden's interception halts a Giants drive, then six plays later, the Falcons get a winning touchdown on a pass from Doug Johnson to Brian Finneran.

CHAPTER SIX

10.20.2002 FALCONS vs. CAROLINA PANTHERS

PLAYING THE PANTHERS

MICHAEL VICK WAS LIKE WATCHING A CARTOON CHARACTER OUT THERE AGAIN. HE'S UNBELIEVABLE.
—PATRICK KERNEY

ATLANTA: After sitting out one game with a shoulder injury, Michael Vick shows why he's the quarterback with a Midas touch. Vick destroys a defense that enters the day as the NFL's second-best, but his statistics are only part of the story.

THERE HE GOES AGAIN
Carolina defensive end Mike Rucker has grabbed Vick's jersey and is about to record a safety in the third quarter when the Falcons franchise cornerstone breaks free, runs to his left, and completes a 21-yard pass over the middle to Shawn Jefferson.

Vick's Houdini act is one of 12 plays on a 79-yard touchdown drive in the third quarter that lasts 9:52. Before T.J. Duckett ends the possession with a 1-yard touchdown run, Vick breaks off a 24-yard run and completes all 6 of his passes.

He ices the game on his final play, a 44-yard run at the end of the third that

Linebackers John Holecek (53) and Mark Simoneau (59) help get the job done against the Panthers, who twice give up the ball on downs. During the course of the afternoon the defense has one interception and forces Carolina to punt six times.

FINAL SCORE:

Falcons **30**   Panthers **0**

Atlanta	3	7	14	6	**30**
Carolina	0	0	0	0	**0**

A shutout of the Panthers gives the Falcons back-to-back victories—and a streak of five consecutive scoreless quarters for the defense.

1st Quarter
Atl–Feely 41 FG
2nd Quarter
Atl–Duckett 7 run (Feely kick)
3rd Quarter
Atl–Duckett 1 run (Feely kick)
Atl–Vick 44 run (Feely kick)
4th Quarter
Atl–Feely 45 FG
Atl–Feely 49 FG

90 ATLANTA FALCONS

Played at Atlanta > > > Attendance: 68,056 > > >

INDIVIDUAL LEADERS RUSHING > Atlanta: *Vick 6-91 1 td* > Carolina: *Fasani 8-58*
PASSING > Atlanta: *Vick 16-22-178* > Carolina: *Fasani 6-18-100 1 int.*
RECEIVING > Atlanta: *Jackson 5-19* > Carolina: *Muhammad 2-21*

begins as a play-action call and unfolds after Vick drops back to pass. Seeing vast holes in the middle of the defense, Vick dashes across the middle of the line of scrimmage and outruns safety Mike Minter down the right sideline.

"The guy was coming so fast that I knew I had a chance to beat him," Vick says. "I knew all I had to do was jab inside him and come back out. He took the bait, and the sideline was my friend. It worked out for me."

Minter moans a familiar refrain.

"If you play tight coverage on him, he'll throw it," he says. "If you play back, he'll run for 30 or 40 yards. It's pretty tough to defend the guy, even tougher to get him down in the backfield."

QUOTE OF THE DAY
"Michael Vick was like watching a cartoon character out there again. He's unbelievable," Patrick Kerney says.

TEAM STATS / 10.20.2002

	Car	Atl
First Downs	12	25
Total Net Yards	205	393
Rushes-Yards	21-101	39-187
Passing Yards	104	206
Passes Comp-Att-Int	9-26-1	20-27-0
Sacked-Yards	4-22	1-8
Penalties-Yards	6-40	9-65
Fumbles-Lost	0-0	2-0
Time of Possession	19:52	40:08

CHAPTER **SIX**

10.27.2002 FALCONS vs. NEW ORLEANS SAINTS

GAME 7: PLAYING THE SAINTS

WHEN THE CHIPS ARE DOWN AND YOU'RE STARING DEFEAT IN THE FACE, THAT'S WHEN QUARTERBACKS ARE MEASURED. —SHAWN JEFFERSON

NEW ORLEANS. Quarterback Aaron Brooks has his fourth-quarter mojo working again, but the Saints learn that a one-point lead won't suffice when Michael Vick gets the ball back with 2:12 remaining.

As all great quarterbacks do, Vick saves his best for last. The 22-year-old phenom helps the Falcons convert four first downs and move 60 yards to set up Jay Feely's 47-yard game-winning field goal as time expires.

COMING-OUT PARTY

Vick overcomes a bruised left shoulder in the first quarter and is so spent on the final drive that he pulls himself from the game.

The Falcons send in backup Doug Johnson to run two plays, but the officiating crew nearly takes the game out of Atlanta's hands. Johnson hands off to Warrick Dunn for no gain at the 29, but the officials allow the Saints to hold the running back on the turf for 22

Placekicker Jay Feely contributes three field goals from 30-yards or beyond, including the game-winner from 47 yards as time expires at the Louisiana Superdome.

92 ATLANTA FALCONS

Played at New Orleans > > > Attendance: 67,883 > > >

INDIVIDUAL LEADERS RUSHING > Atlanta: *Dunn 23-142 1 td* > New Orleans: *McAllister 17-115 2 tds*
PASSING > Atlanta: *Vick 16-24-195* > New Orleans: *Brooks 16-35-192 2 tds, 2 int.*
RECEIVING > Atlanta: *Dunn 5-28* > New Orleans: *Horn 5-61 1 td*

FINAL SCORE:
Falcons **37** *Saints* **35**

Atlanta	0	14	10	13	**37**
New Orleans	10	0	15	10	**35**

The Falcons gain nearly 100 yards more than the Saints, but the first meeting of the season between these NFC South rivals is decided on the game's final play.

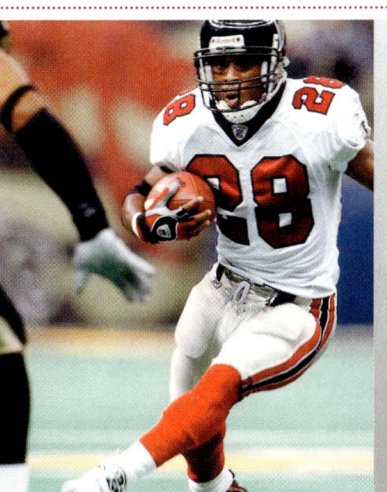

1st Quarter
NO–Carney 40 FG
NO–McAllister 1 run (Carney kick)

2nd Quarter
Atl–Vick 3 run (Feely kick)
Atl–Dunn 3 run (Feely kick)

3rd Quarter
Atl–Christian 8 run (Feely kick)
NO–McAllister 19 pass from Brooks (Brooks-Williams pass)
Atl–Feely 31 FG
NO–Horn 6 pass from Brooks (Carney kick)

4th Quarter
Atl–Feely 32 FG
Atl–Vick 32 run (Feely kick)
NO–Carney 40 FG
NO–McAllister 16 run (Carney kick)
Atl–Feely 47 FG

Warrick Dunn leads the team in rushes and receptions against the Saints.

seconds. When Johnson finally spikes the ball to stop the clock, the Falcons have only 3 seconds for Feely to kick the game-winner.

Vick, exhausted, watches the field goal attempt kneeling on the sideline. Feely's kick is good, and everyone joins in a midfield celebration.

QUOTE OF THE DAY
"When the chips are down and you're staring defeat in the face, that's when quarterbacks are measured. You find out what type of leader they are, what type of quarterback they are, find out where their guts are, you find out where their heart is," receiver Shawn Jefferson, a 12-year pro, says of Vick.

TEAM STATS 10.27.2002

	Atl	NO
First Downs	28	22
Total Net Yards	446	351
Rushes-Yards	38-260	24-159
Passing Yards	186	192
Passes Comp-Att-Int	16-25-0	16-35-2
Sacked-Yards	3-9	0-0
Penalties-Yards	10-85	9-96
Fumbles-Lost	2-2	2-1
Time of Possession	35:03	24:57

CHAPTER SIX

11.03.2002   FALCONS vs. *BALTIMORE RAVENS*

PLAYING THE RAVENS

WE GOT THROUGH. WE PERSEVERED. IT WAS TOUGH. —MICHAEL VICK

ATLANTA. Patrick Kerney always thought the law of averages would even out for his team. He scores the Falcons first defensive touchdown in 38 games with a 4-yard run after the fumble recovery and Kerney puts Atlanta on course for an ugly win, but the fourth-year defensive end doesn't care about aesthetics.

"It was a sloppy performance," Kerney says. "We gave up too many yards and too many big plays."

Yes, they do, but the Falcons (5-3) also win their fourth straight game to remain in the hunt for their first playoff appearance since 1998. Jay Feely ends the scoring with a 40-yard field goal late in the third quarter.

NO NEED FOR SUPERMAN

Quarterback Michael Vick struggles from start to finish. The 22-year-old, who leads the NFL with 9.0 yards per

Let's hear it for team defense —five Falcons work together to bring down Baltimore's Jamal Lewis, who finishes with just 36 yards rushing.

TEAM STATS   11.03.2002

	Bal	Atl
First Downs	15	14
Total Net Yards	340	241
Rushes-Yards	24-153	34-126
Passing Yards	187	115
Passes Comp-Att-Int	14-28-1	12-24-1
Sacked-Yards	6-42	3-21
Penalties-Yards	7-62	4-33
Fumbles-Lost	2-1	2-0
Time of Possession	28:18	31:42

Played at Atlanta > > > Attendance: 68,532 > > >

INDIVIDUAL LEADERS RUSHING > Atlanta: *Duckett 13-75 1 td* > Baltimore: *Lewis 12-36*
PASSING > Atlanta: *Vick 12-24-136 1 int.* > Baltimore: *Blake 14-27-229 1 tds, 1 int.*
RECEIVING > Atlanta: *Finneran 3-42* > Baltimore: *T. Taylor 4-127 1 td*

FINAL SCORE:

Falcons **20** Ravens **17**

Atlanta	3	14	3	0	**20**
Baltimore	3	7	7	0	**17**

1st Quarter
Bal–Stover 32 FG
Atl–Feely 23 FG

2nd Quarter
Atl–Kerney 4-yd. fumble return (Feely kick)
Atl–Duckett 1 run (Feely kick)
Bal–T. Taylor 7 pass from Blake (Stover kick)

3rd Quarter
Bal–Ricard 19 run (Stover kick)
Atl–Feely 40 FG

carry and last week became the first quarterback in league history to run for 90 or more yards in consecutive games, has minus 5 yards rushing on seven carries.

Vick also fumbles twice and throws his first interception of the season, ending the third-longest streak in franchise history with 171 straight passes, dating back to the 2001 season finale. He completes just 12 of 24 passes for 136 yards and a 50.0 quarterback rating that's 43.4 points off his season mark, which was second-best in the NFC.

MIXING IT UP
Coach Dan Reeves unleashes some unconventional plays to ice the game.
"That's going after the win," Dunn says.

Continued on page 97

Falcons fans expect to see Patrick Kerney making a sack, but seeing No. 97 score a touchdown is a bigger thrill.

CHAPTER **SIX**

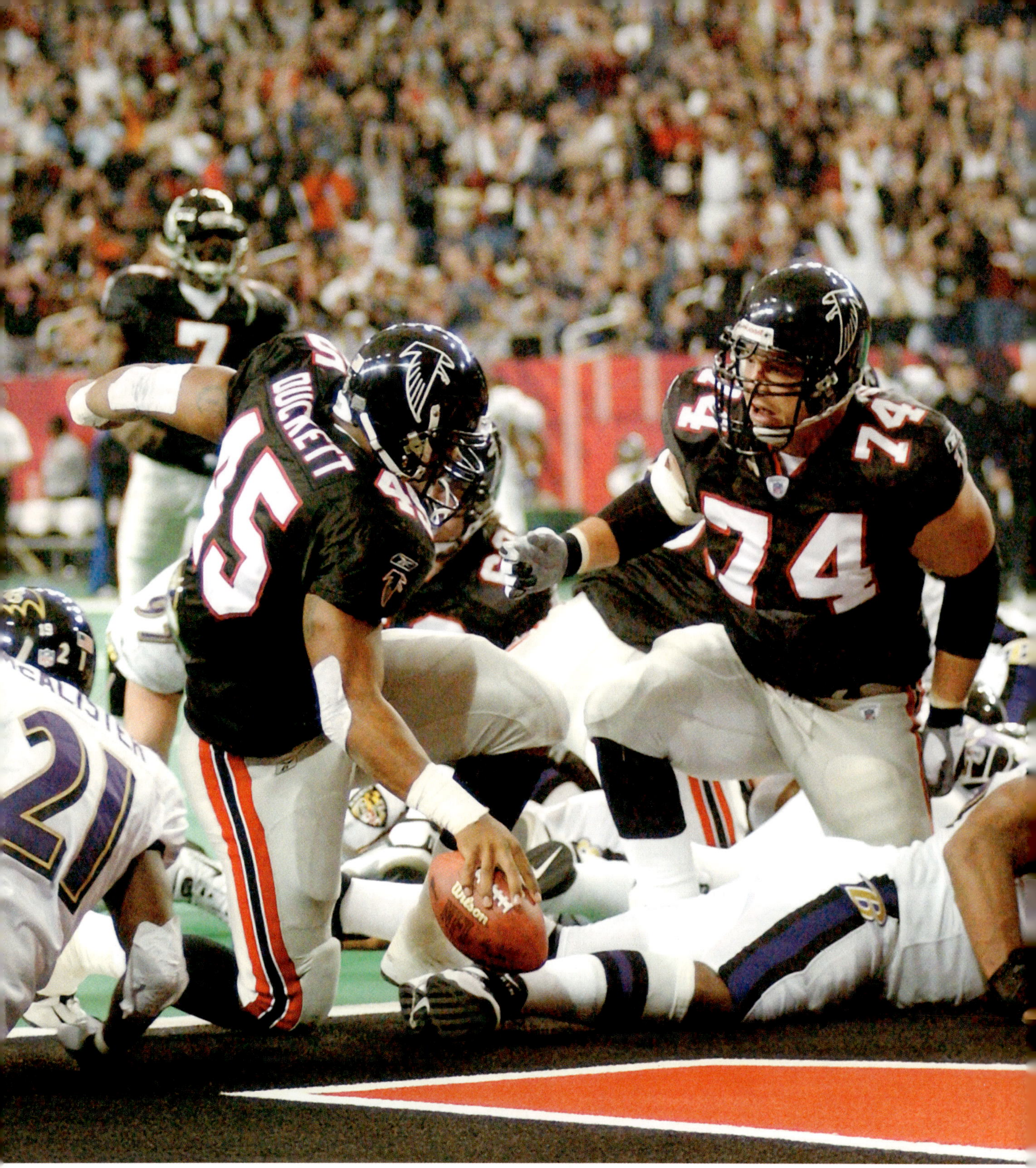
DUCKETT
45
74

Continued from page 95

QUOTE OF THE DAY

"We got through. We persevered. It was tough. I think we kind of underestimated them a little bit, thinking we were going to come out and beat them. They played a great game. One thing you've got to realize is they're professionals too," says Vick.

Trevor Gaylor's big game against the Ravens at the Georgia Dome includes four receptions for 32 yards. One of his catches comes on a fourth down at the Baltimore 31 with 2 minutes remaining and the Falcons trying to run out the clock. "I was almost sure we wouldn't go for it," Gaylor says afterward. "The play calling in the fourth quarter—wow! When our backs were to the wall, it worked to perfection. For Dan Reeves to throw it on fourth-and-4 was really shocking."

The Falcons defense delivers again, holding Baltimore to just two touchdowns as Atlanta improves to 5-3. The Ravens are without No. 1 quarterback Chris Redman, and backup Jeff Blake completes just 12 of 24 passes, is intercepted once, is sacked six times, and fumbles at his own 4-yard line.

CHAPTER SIX

CHAPTER SEVEN
CLOUD OF DUST
2002 REGULAR SEASON—GAMES 9-10

11.10.2002   FALCONS vs. *PITTSBURGH STEELERS*

PLAYING THE STEELERS

MORE FOURTH-QUARTER MAGIC FROM MICHAEL VICK AND SOME TOUGH DEFENSE KEEP THE FALCONS IN THE HUNT AT THE SEASON'S HALFWAY POINT.

PITTSBURGH. Game nine leaves Atlanta feeling uplifted, depressed, happy, and hurt. What transpires—the first NFL tie since 1997 and the Falcons first since 1986—is hard to fathom. Both teams enter with four straight victories and five wins in their last six games. Over the course of the afternoon as Tommy Maddox and Plaxico Buress continue to write their names in the Pittsburgh record books, the Steelers take a 34-17 lead on Todd Peterson's 34-yard field goal with 12:34 remaining. The Falcons go three-and-out, and all appears lost.

FOURTH QUARTER DOMINO EFFECT
Chris Mohr punts from the Atlanta 33, but the Falcons recover the loose ball at the Steelers 37 after Mark Simoneau and Brian Kozlowski force Antwaan Randle El to fumble away the return. Brian Finneran catches a 15-yard pass, and Michael Vick runs for 12 to set up Bob Christian's 1-yard run. With 7:44 remaining, Pittsburgh leads 34-24.

After the Steelers go three-and-out, the Falcons put together an 11-play, 43-yard scoring drive that includes two stunning third-down conversions. Vick faces third-and-9 at the Atlanta 36 when he eludes pressure long enough to hit Alge Crumpler for a 21-yard gain down the left side. Vick converts a third-and-

Continued on page 101

Michael Vick has a busy game with a season-high 24 completions and a season-high 46 attempts. He rushes for 52 yards and a touchdown, but passes for nearly 300 yards against Pittsburgh.

98   ATLANTA FALCONS

The Steelers have trouble slowing Shawn Jefferson and the Falcons. Vick and Jefferson hook up on nine passes for 131 yards and one touchdown at Heinz Field.

Played at Pittsburgh > > > Attendance: 62,779 > > >

INDIVIDUAL LEADERS : RUSHING > Atlanta: *Dunn 20-129 1 td* > Pittsburgh: *Zereoue 37-123*
PASSING > Atlanta: *Vick 46-24-294 1 td* > Pittsburgh: *Maddox 41-28-473 4 tds, 1 int.*
RECEIVING > Atlanta: *Jefferson 9-131 1 td* > Pittsburgh: *Ward 11-139 1 td*

FINAL SCORE: (OT)

Falcons 34 — Steelers 34

Atlanta	0	7	10	17	0	**34**
Pittsburgh	3	14	14	3	0	**34**

1st Quarter
Pit–Peterson 34 FG

2nd Quarter
Atl–Jefferson 43 pass from Vick (Feely kick)
Pit–Burress 33 pass from Maddox (Peterson kick)
Pit–Ward 5 pass from Maddox (Peterson kick)

3rd Quarter
Atl–Dunn 59 run (Feely kick)
Pit–Burress 62 pass from Maddox (kick blocked)
Atl–Feely 36 FG
Pit–Tuman 18 pass from Maddox (Maddox-Ward pass)

4th Quarter
Pit–Peterson 34 FG
Atl–Christian 1 run (Feely kick)
Atl–Feely 40 FG
Atl–Vick 11 run (Feely kick)

Defensive end Brady Smith is all tied up on this play, just like the Falcons and Steelers finished on this afternoon in Pittsburgh. Atlanta battles back after trailing 31-17 after three quarters. The Falcons scored 17 points in the final 11 minutes to take the game into overtime.

CHAPTER **SEVEN**

UNTIL THE FALCONS AND STEELERS REACH THE OVERTIME PERIOD, NEITHER DEFENSE CAN STOP THE OPPOSING OFFENSE. MICHAEL VICK FINISHES WITH 346 YARDS OF OFFENSE, WHILE PITTSBURGH'S TOMMY MADDOX PASSES FOR 473 YARDS.

Continued from page 98

24 by connecting with Shawn Jefferson for a 35-yard pass. Jay Feely kicks a 40-yard field goal three plays later to bring the Falcons within 7 at the 2:26 mark.

TIED DOWN

In leading the Falcons to 17 unanswered points in the fourth quarter, Vick completes 7 of 13 passes for 120 yards and runs three times for 30 yards, including his spectacular last-minute touchdown scramble with 42 seconds left to drive the game into overtime. But neither team can score in the extra period and the game ends in a heartwrenching tie.

Nose tackle Ed Jasper (95) and the defense hold the Steelers scoreless on four possessions in overtime.

42 SECONDS LEFT:

"I came in the huddle and I told the guys, 'Ride on my back, and hear what I'm about to do. I'm going to make it happen. Everybody do their assignments and everybody stay together,'" Michael Vick says when the drive starts. Four plays later, with 42 seconds left, Atlanta stands second-and-10 at the 11. Vick scrambles right, then breaks left and weaves his way past cornerback Dewayne Washington to the end zone. He runs farther horizontally than vertically to force overtime.

"With Michael you're never out of a game," coach Dan Reeves says. "It motivates everybody. It motivates your defense. Mike's going to give us a chance to win."

TEAM STATS 11.10.2002

	Atl	Pit
First Downs	21	30
Total Net Yards	447	645
Rushes-Yards	31-168	42-182
Passing Yards	279	463
Passes Comp-Att-Int	24-46-0	28-41-1
Sacked-Yards	3-15	2-10
Penalties-Yards	11-95	4-25
Fumbles-Lost	2-2	2-2
Time of Possession	35:10	39:50

CHAPTER **SEVEN**

I'm no different from anyone else who's experienced a major loss in his life.

Warrick

God doesn't lay a burden on those who can't handle it. —Warrick Dunn

Dunn, a two-time Pro Bowl selection in Tampa Bay, lands in Atlanta to contribute as a rusher and receiver.

Warrick Dunn's entire adult life is rooted in the news he received in January 1993, only a few days after his 18th birthday and just before he was to make a recruiting visit to Florida State. His mother, Betty Smothers, 36, a police officer in their hometown of Baton Rouge, La., had been murdered while helping a merchant make a late-night deposit. She needed the second job to help raise Warrick, her oldest child, and five others. No linebacker could slam Dunn this hard. The good people of Baton Rouge raised $200,000 to

WARRICK **DUNN** Running back

Drafted in the first round by the Tampa Bay Bucs in 1997, Dunn is a formidable weapon in the Falcons arsenal.

CHAPTER **SEVEN**   103

keep his siblings fed, clothed, housed, and educated. Dunn did what his mother had always wanted: He went to Florida State, stayed focused on his goals, and graduated in four years.

Dunn became the legal guardian of his three brothers and two sisters. To this day, he doesn't complain. In any interview the two-time Pro Bowler takes a long pause before answering the first question. Reporters trying to probe into his personal life will only get so far.

ON OR OFF THE FIELD WARRICK DUNN GIVES 100 PERCENT. HELPING OTHERS IS HIS WAY OF HONORING HIS MOTHER'S MEMORY.

"I'm no different from anyone else who's experienced a major loss in his life," Dunn says. "God doesn't lay a burden on those who can't handle it." Dunn admits he's thankful for time, the great equalizer; for love, the great healer; and above all else for God. He also is quick to point out that he's been blessed financially beyond his wildest dreams.

Dunn knows that his mother would want him to share his wealth with people less fortunate. So he has expanded his Warrick Dunn Foundation from Tampa Bay to Atlanta. His program, "Homes for the Holidays" identifies young single mothers who are strong enough to maintain a permanent residence but need a financial push to take that first step. The foundation partners with real estate agencies, corporations, retailers, and local and state governments around the Southeast to fully furnish and stock new homes every Thanksgiving.

Dunn makes the downpayment on the mortgage and covers closing costs and other expenses. "For me, this is easier than football," Dunn says with a soft smile. "To give back to these people is easy."

Warrick Dunn flashes a stiff arm, dashes through opposing defensive lines, and outruns opponents to the end zone. In his first season with the Falcons, Dunn gets 280 touches—250 rushes and 30 receptions—and totals 1,304 yards of offense. Equally important, the threat he poses in Atlanta's backfield provides quarterback Michael Vick room to maneuver. Dunn finishes the season second on the team in scoring, with nine touchdowns, behind only fieldgoal kicker Jay Feely.

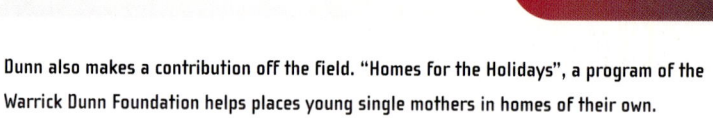

2002 INDIVIDUAL STATS / Warrick Dunn

Rushes	230
Rushing yards	927
Longest run	59 yds.
Receiving yards	377
Touchdowns	9

28

Dunn also makes a contribution off the field. "Homes for the Holidays", a program of the Warrick Dunn Foundation helps places young single mothers in homes of their own.

104 ATLANTA FALCONS

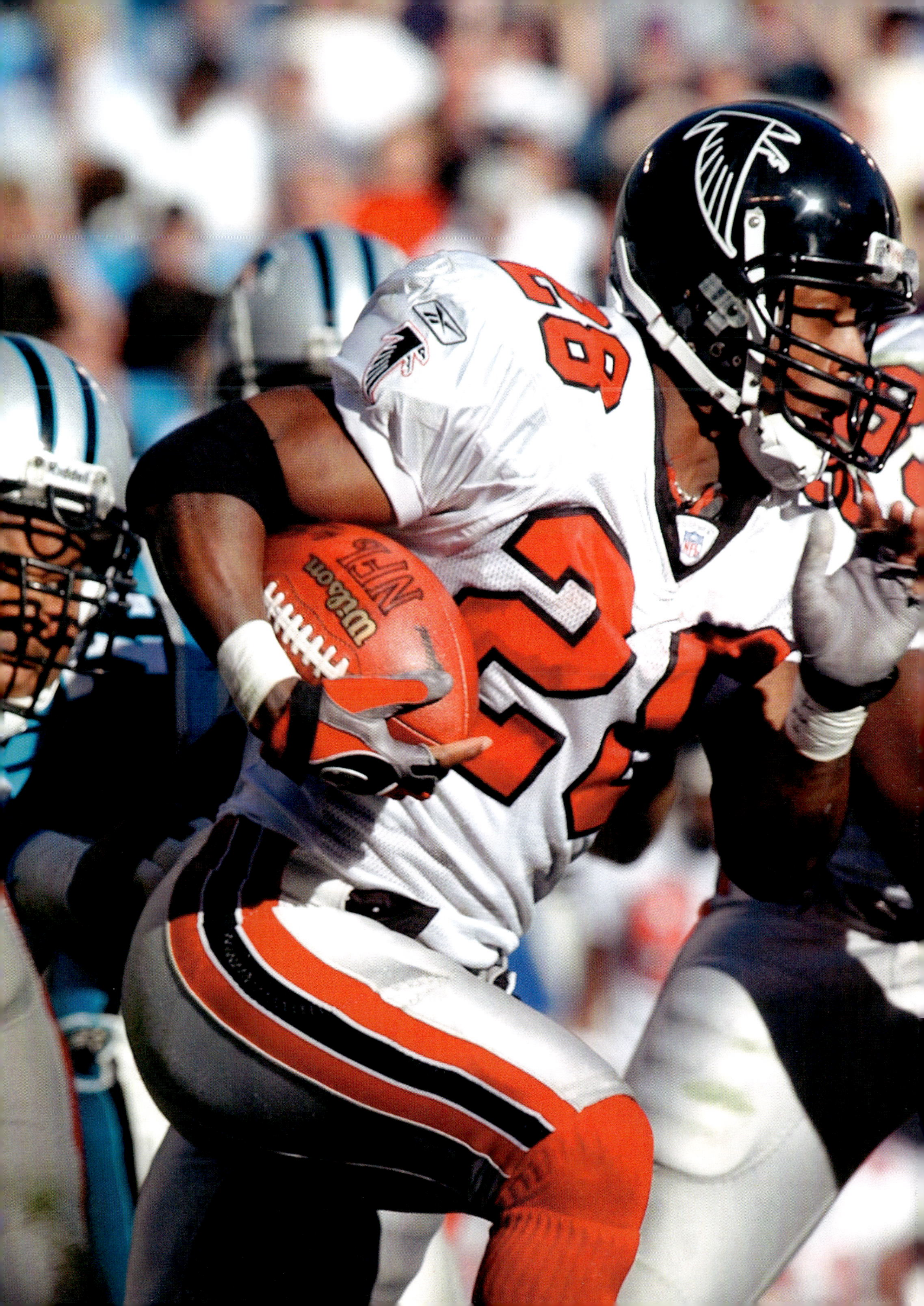
Wilson
NFL

GAME 10

11.17.2002   FALCONS vs. NEW ORLEANS SAINTS

PLAYING THE SAINTS

MICHAEL VICK AIRS IT OUT AND THE FALCONS REMAIN A TEAM ON THE MOVE—TOWARD THE PLAY-OFFS—AS THEY SLIP PAST THE SAINTS AND EXTEND THEIR UNBEATEN STREAK TO SIX GAMES.

ATLANTA. Michael Vick's cache of weapons is well-known. Arguably the fastest quarterback in NFL history, the Atlanta Falcons 22-year-old phenom can use his arm as a cannon when necessary. He proves he can fly too by diving for a third-quarter touchdown.

Vick doesn't need to save his best effort for the final seconds in beating the New Orleans Saints for the second time in four weeks. In fact, the 24-17 victory, which improves Atlanta's winning streak to six games, is decided when Vick's 4-yard touchdown pass to Alge Crumpler gives the Falcons a 14-point lead with 3:56 remaining.

NICE RECOVERY

The Atlanta defense plays a considerable role too. New Orleans running back Deuce McAllister is held to a season-low 43 yards rushing before leaving early in the fourth quarter with a sprained right ankle.

Vick's second cousin, Saints quarterback Aaron Brooks, completes 20 of 31 passes

Fullback Bob Christian opens the holes for Dunn and Vick. Trevor Gaylor starts the scoring with a 74-yard TD catch in the second period. The second-largest crowd in Falcons history (70,382) watch the Falcons sweep New Orleans.

106   ATLANTA FALCONS

Played at Atlanta > > > Attendance: 70,382 > > >

INDIVIDUAL LEADERS: RUSHING > Atlanta: *Dunn 26-90* > New Orleans: *McAllister 13-43*
PASSING > Atlanta: *Vick 11-23-160 2 tds, 1 int.* > New Orleans: *Brooks 20-31-279 2 tds, 1 int.*
RECEIVING > Atlanta: *Gaylor 3-100 1 td* > New Orleans: *Horn 3-134 1 td*

FINAL SCORE:

Falcons **24** — Saints **17**

Atlanta	0	7	7	10	**24**
New Orleans	0	0	3	14	**17**

2nd Quarter
Atl–Gaylor 74 pass from Vick (Feely kick)

3rd Quarter
Atl–Vick 7 run (Feely kick)
NO–Carney 35 FG

4th Quarter
Atl–Feely 42 FG
NO–Horn 57 pass from Brooks (Carney kick)
Atl–Crumpler 4 pass from Vick (Feely kick)
NO–Stallworth 12 pass from Brooks (Carney kick)

Second-year tight end Alge Crumpler again shows he can make big plays. In the fourth quarter, he hauls in a 4-yard pass from Vick for the winning touchdown, lifting the Falcons past quarterback Aaron Brooks and New Orleans.

for 279 yards and goes 11-for-15 with 168 yards in the fourth quarter. But a fourth-quarter interception leads to the Falcons final score and forces New Orleans to play catch-up.

IN A ZONE
Dunn carries the Falcons rushing attack for the third time in four weeks, gaining 90 yards on 26 carries, and Jay Feely hits one of two field-goal attempts — the second giving Atlanta a 17-3 lead.

But the spotlight is on Vick, whose 74-yard touchdown pass to Trevor Gaylor in the second quarter and diving touchdown in the third set the tone.

QUOTE OF THE DAY:
"I saw him point deep. If he says, 'Go deep,' I believe him, because he'll embarrass you. He can throw it far," says Trevor Gaylor.

TEAM STATS 11.17.2002

	NO	Atl
First Downs	16	22
Total Net Yards	343	292
Rushes-Yards	21-80	37-155
Passing Yards	263	137
Passes Comp-Att-Int	20-31-1	11-23-1
Sacked-Yards	3-16	3-23
Penalties-Yards	16-133	9-70
Fumbles-Lost	1-1	0-0
Time of Possession	26:37	33:23

CHAPTER **SEVEN** 107

CHAPTER EIGHT
PASS THE MAGIC
2002 REGULAR SEASON—GAMES 11-12

11.24.2002   FALCONS vs. CAROLINA PANTHERS

PLAYING THE PANTHERS

PULLING OFF A SEASON SWEEP OF THE PANTHERS MAKES FOR A GREAT ROAD TRIP AND GIVES THE FALCONS A 7-GAME UNBEATEN STREAK AND ATLANTA'S MAGICAL SEASON CONTINUES.

CHARLOTTE. Atlanta becomes the first team to shut out a division opponent twice in the same year since Denver did so to San Diego in 1976. The Falcons, improving their unbeaten streak to seven games, maintain the sixth spot in the NFC playoff race.

Safety Keion Carpenter is the first player to pass the magic in Charlotte. Breaking on Rodney Peete's soft pass to Muhsin Muhammad early in the first quarter, Carpenter grabs the ball and runs down the left sideline for a 41-yard touchdown and a 7-0 lead.

Carpenter instantly drops into "pass the magic" position – hind end down, knees bent, back straight, head level, arms forward, and fingers wiggling— so he can give his good luck to another teammate. "Pass the magic" is a little gimmick Ray Buchanan worked up in training camp to celebrate a good play.

"Pass the magic, man," Buchanan says. "That's what we do."

SCORING MACHINE
Runs by Warrick Dunn and T.J. Duckett give the team a total of 19 rushing touchdowns to set a franchise record. The previous mark of 18 was set in 1973 and tied in '98. The 2000 Falcons ran for six TDs all season.

Safety Johndale Carty whoops it up after his interception and 37-yard return against the Panthers. Atlanta's defense holds Carolina to 122 yards, records eight sacks, and forces six turnovers.

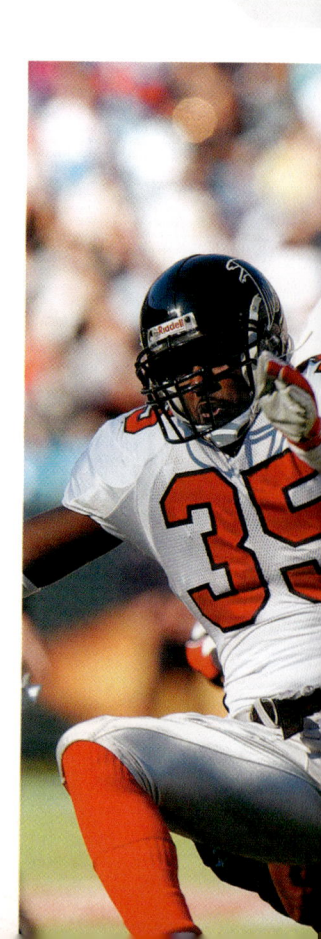

108   ATLANTA FALCONS

It's another Carolina Crunch ... and another Atlanta shutout of the Panthers. In this November road game, the Falcons give up just 122 yards, while their offense rolls up 426 yards. The Falcons defense gets things moving for the offense. Keion Carpenter's 41-yard interception return gives Atlanta a 7-0 lead.

Played at Charlotte > > > Attendance: 72,533 > > >

INDIVIDUAL LEADERS
RUSHING > Atlanta: *Duckett* 22-66 yds > Carolina: *Brown* 4-29yds
PASSING > Atlanta: *Vick* 24-19-272yds 2 tds > Carolina: *Peete* 6-11-64 yds. 2 ints.
RECEIVING > Atlanta: *Finneran* 4-104 yds > Carolina: *Hoover* 3-46 yds

FINAL SCORE:

Falcons **41** — Panthers **0**

Atlanta	14	14	13	0	**41**
Carolina	0	0	0	0	**0**

1st Quarter
Atl-Carpenter 41 interception (Feely kick)
Atl-Dunn 31 pass from Vick (Feely Kick)

2nd Quarter
Atl-Dunn 5 run (Feely kick)
Atl-Duckett 1 run (Feely kick)

3rd Quarter
Atl-Crumpler 4 pass from Vick (Feely kick)
Atl-Gaylor 5 pass from Johnson (Feely kick failed)

It's a laugher for Michael Vick, who passes for 272 yards and 2 TDs. Linebacker Keith Brooking turns into a ball carrier after his interception. The Falcons 41-0 shutout was their biggest margin of victory since a 41-0 victory over San Diego in 1973.

CHAPTER **EIGHT** 109

The scoring starts with safety Keion Carpenter picking off a pass and taking it 41 yards for a touchdown. The score means it's "pass the magic time" for the Falcons.

DAY AT THE OFFICE
Though his performance isn't necessarily superhuman, Vick is nonetheless sensational. He completes 19 of 24 passes for 272 yards, two touchdowns, and a career-best 141.7 rating.

The Atlanta line allows no sacks to a Carolina pass rush that leads the NFL with 35. Vick avoids being sacked for the first time in 12 career starts.

YOUR TURN
Doug Johnson replaces Vick at the end of the third quarter and attempts only one pass, but it's a good one. A 5-yard touchdown to Trevor Gaylor, which ends the scoring.

QUOTE OF THE DAY
Buchanan believes the Panthers quit trying in the second quarter.

"Man, once it was about 21-0, I could look in their eyes and say, 'Man, these cats are dead. They're just waiting for somebody to bring a shovel out and bury them,' " he says.

TEAM STATS — 11.24.2002

	Atl	Car
First Downs	25	10
Total Net Yards	426	122
Rushes-Yards	47-146	14-71
Passing Yards	277	51
Passes Comp-Att-Int	25-20-0	26-13-4
Sacked-Yards	0-0	8-64
Penalties-Yards	6-65	5-39
Fumbles-Lost	1-1	3-2
Time of Possession	39:48	20:12

Victory No. 2 over Carolina was a joint effort. T.J. Duckett and the offense scored at will, and the defense put points on the board too. "That was as close to a perfect game as you can possibly play," cornerback Ray Buchanan says. "The defense frustrated them and kept them from scoring any points. We met our goal of shutting them out again. And Mike, the Magic Man, had our offense rolling." The Falcons are feeling something a coach can't teach—the overwhelming desire to win.

CHAPTER EIGHT 111

KEITH BRO

I feel like I play the run as well as anybody in

KEITH **BROOKING** — Linebacker

Born in Senoia, Georgia, Keith has been a Falcon since he was drafted in 1998. Local boy makes good. A fifth-year pro, Brooking has been a Pro Bowl pick in each of the past two seasons.

the NFL, but there are still a lot of things I can do to improve. —Keith Brooking

*I*t's late September and the Falcons have a bye week. Near Thomson, Ga., some 30 miles west of Augusta, Keith Brooking has joined quarterback Doug Johnson to go hunting on private land owned by punter Chris Mohr. Dove season has just opened in Georgia, but these guys aim to bag a deer. It's no secret that Brooking loves the hunt—on and off the field. "It's awesome," Brooking says, "a great opportunity to get away from football and let your mind wander."

CHAPTER *EIGHT*   113

Born in Georgia, leading tackler Keith Brooking is a lifelong Falcons fan. "I grew up watching Jessie Tuggle play and all of a sudden I get to the locker room and his locker was next to mine," Brooking says. "That was pretty special. Everything I've taken from him is positive." In 2002 Keith Brooking ranks second in the NFL in tackles with 111, just behind Chicago's Brian Urlacher's 117. He's also dedicated to helping the community. He was nominated for USA Weekend Magazine's "Most Caring Athlete" award and a "Good Guys" award by the Sporting News.

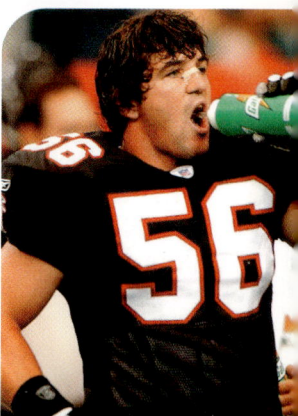

A 26-year-old native of Senoia, Ga., Brooking grew up southeast of Atlanta and starred at East Coweta High School before signing a letter of intent at Georgia Tech. He was the school's all-time leading tackler.

Brooking's Georgia Tech teams never won more than seven games in his last three years. As a rookie and first-round draft pick with the Falcons, Brooking played behind Cornelius Bennett. It was in November 2000 when torn ligaments at the base of his toes ended Brooking's season after five games.

I'LL BE HUNTING LONG AFTER MY FOOTBALL CAREER IS OVER; IT DEFINITELY PROVIDES ME WITH A RELEASE. —KEITH BROOKING

"I was only that much more eager to come back and prove to everybody that I was as good as ever and working as hard as possible to get better," Brooking says.

The 2002 season ends with Brooking's selection to a second straight Pro Bowl, though this time he's not going as an alternate. He's a first-teamer who ends the year with 98 solo tackles, tops in the NFL. He's also a deer hunter who intends to keep hunting.

"I'll be hunting long after my football career is over," Brooking says with a grin. "It definitely provides me with a release, I guess you could say."

2002 INDIVIDUAL STATS — Keith Brooking

Starts	16
Total tackles	212
Solo tackles	100
Assists	112
Interceptions	2
Yards	24
Fumbles recovered	2

#56

GAME 12

12.01.2002 FALCONS vs. MINNESOTA VIKINGS

PLAYING THE VIKINGS

IT'S THE THIRD OVERTIME GAME OF THE REGULAR SEASON FOR ATLANTA, AND THIS TIME THE FALCONS GET IT RIGHT, THANKS TO A BIG PLAY FROM MICHAEL. HIS SPECTACULAR OVERTIME SPRINT TO THE END ZONE MAKES FOR A HAPPY ENDING.

MINNEAPOLIS. Michael Vick shatters a 51-year-old NFL record for rushing by a quarterback with a 173-yard performance that pushes the Falcons' unbeaten streak to eight games. Vick overcomes two lost fumbles and an interception by throwing a 39-yard touchdown pass, running for a 28-yard score, and breaking off a 46-yard scramble that ends the day and defies NFL laws of nature.

Vick wants to compensate after a fumble on a handoff and another when the ball is stripped from behind in the second quarter. The Vikings sprint ahead, 14-7. But Brian Finneran, who catches five passes for 114 yards, ties the score at 14-14 with a 39-yard reception with 37 seconds remaining before intermission.

Michael Bennett puts the Vikings on top, 21-14 late in the third, but Vick answers with a five-play drive in which he runs three times for 60 yards. His 28-yard touchdown, coming out of a

Vick accounts for 346 of the Falcons 379 yards on offense. His 46-yard run with 11 seconds left in overtime helps Atlanta continue its eight-game unbeaten streak. Despite a bad snap, placekicker Jay Feely and holder Chris Mohr combine to get three points on a 44-yard, fourth-quarter field goal.

116 ATLANTA FALCONS

Played at Minneapolis > > > Attendance: 63,947 > > >

INDIVIDUAL LEADERS: RUSHING > Atlanta: *Vick 10-173 2 tds* > Minnesota: *Bennett 18-86 1 td*
PASSING > Atlanta: *Vick 28-11-173 1 td, 1 int.* > Minnesota: *Culpepper 43-23-266 1 td, 3 ints.*
RECEIVING > Atlanta: *Finneran 5-114 1 td* > Minnesota: *Moss 9-134*

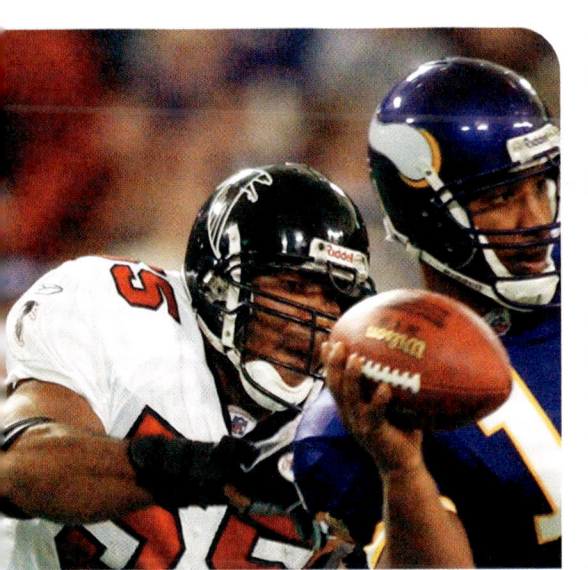

Power-I formation with two tight ends, begins with a fake handoff to Bob Christian. The fullback, as designed, runs right, and Vick breaks left to even the score.

BACK AND FORTH

Jay Feely's 44-yard field goal with 3:53 remaining gives the Falcons their first lead at 24-21, but it's punter Chris Mohr who keeps the play alive. Mohr, Feely's holder, takes a snap that bounces off the turf and in a split second gets the ball upright and spins the seams of the ball away from the kicker's right foot.

The Atlanta defense, which sacks Daunte Culpepper six times, catches a huge break with 20 seconds remaining after receiver Randy Moss takes a handoff and throws a 6-yard touchdown pass to Culpepper. The play is nullified when rookie left tackle Bryant McKinnie fails to report as an eligible receiver. Minnesota settles for Gary Anderson's 29-yard field goal, which forces Atlanta's third overtime this year.

Linebacker John Thierry (55) has Vikings quarterback Daunte Culpepper in his sights all day long, sacking him once. The rest of the Falcons keep the pressure on as well. Atlanta records six sacks over the course of the game.

FINAL SCORE: (OT)

Falcons **30** — *Vikings* **24**

Atlanta	0	14	7	3	6	**30**
Minnesota	7	7	7	3	0	**24**

1st Quarter
Min–Culpepper 1 run (Anderson kick)

2nd Quarter
Atl–Christian 1 run (Feely kick)
Min–Goodwin 2 pass from Culpepper (Anderson kick)
Atl–Finneran 39 pass from Vick (Feely kick)

3rd Quarter
Min–Bennett 1 run (Anderson kick)
Atl–Vick 28 run (Feely kick)

4th Quarter
Atl–Feely 44 FG
Min–Anderson 29 FG

Overtime
Atl–Vick 46 run

TEAM STATS / 12.01.2002

	Atl	Min
First Downs	19	21
Total Net Yards	379	369
Rushes-Yards	29-227	32-139
Passing Yards	152	230
Passes Comp-Att-Int	11-28-1	23-43-3
Sacked-Yards	2-21	6-36
Penalties-Yards	5-34	10-95
Fumbles-Lost	2-2	1-0
Time of Possession	25:40	36:45

CHAPTER EIGHT

Nose tackle Ed Jasper takes Culpepper to the Metrodome turf. The Falcons ring up six sacks, helping run their undefeated streak to eight games. Atlanta's defense makes Duarte Culpepper's life difficult in overtime too. Back-to-back sacks force the Vikings to punt.

VICK'S 46-YARD MIRACLE RUN

Overtimes this season seem to be part of the Falcons gameplan. Vick is looking for a quick win and a happier finish than Pittsburgh.

T.J. Duckett gains 2 yards before Vick rolls left on a pass play and finds a gap he can exploit. "The guy turned his back who had man-to-man coverage, and I said, 'I might as well take off with it,'" Vick says. "So I took off with it and broke through the middle, and two guys had me from the angle. I tried to outrun them and I did."

Everything he does overshadows the best efforts of Culpepper (266 yards passing), Bennett (186 rushing), and super star receiver Moss (134 receiving).

"Unbelievable," Finneran says. "They play that song 'Super Freak' for Randy Moss. They should've put it back on after Michael's run."

Until Vick changes the record book for yards rushing by a quarterback with 173, the crown belonged to Green Bay's Tobin Rote, who had 150 in a 1951 effort against Chicago. Since the 1970 NFL-AFL the record was held by the Bears Bobby Douglas, who rushed for 127 yards against Oakland in 1972.

Michael Vick's shoes are now on display in the NFL Football Hall of Fame.

Atlanta tight end Reggie Kelly (89) beats the Vikings defense for a pair of catches that total 13 yards. For the first time in three overtime games in the 2002 season, Atlanta pulls out a victory.

118 ATLANTA FALCONS

PASSING THE MAGIC—
THE DEFENSE

The Falcons defense is coming together.

Defensive coordinator Wade Phillips loves Texas. If time allows, he'll lean back in a chair and get in a few plugs about his cattle ranch outside Austin and about his legendary father, Bum Phillips. Most NFL head coaches and defensive coordinators have little time to enjoy the finer things in life like livestock.

Such is the case with Phillips in March 2003 as he looks toward the coming season. He knows he did a good job of resurrecting the Falcons defense in 2002. "We weren't loaded personnel-wise, and we didn't have the most money in the world to spend on defense." Progress, however, was made.

- Switching from a 4-3 alignment to a 3-4 front, Phillips returns six starters from the previous year—linebacker Keith Brooking, ends Patrick Kerney and Brady Smith, strong safety Gerald McBurrows, and cornerbacks Ray Buchanan and Ashley Ambrose.
- With major assists from Ed Jasper, Ellis Johnson, Matt Stewart, Juran Bolden, Chris Draft, Keion Carpenter, and Sam Rogers, the defense buys into Phillips' plan. The Falcons end the regular season having jumped 16 spots in scoring defense to eighth and 14 spots in pass defense to 16th.
- The 2002 defense dramatically improves in completion percentage allowed, dropping their average percentage to 55.4 and moving from 31st to fourth. Takeaways soar from 30, tied for 17th, to 39, second best in the NFL. Sacks improve from 37 to 47 leaving Atlanta tied for fourth among league leaders.

"I never have gone for, 'It's going to take us two or three years once we get the system down,' " Phillips says. "I've always put it on the coaches and said, 'We're going to get them ready to play.' You can't say, 'Gosh, well, they haven't learned it yet.' I mean it isn't rocket science."

Phillips is liking his chances for 2003—a combination of veterans such as Keith Brooking, John Holecek, and Sam Rogers and some younger faces are a solid base to build on.

Quickly adjusting to the 3-4 defensive alignment, Wade Phillips' defense picked up the pace in 2002 and intends to do it again in 2003. During Atlanta's eight-game unbeaten streak, defense makes a difference. The Falcons have five victories decided by seven points or less, win two more by shutouts, and settle for one tie.

CHAPTER **EIGHT**

THE RUN

Michael Vick generates some overtime magic in Minnesota on a scrambling 7.3 second touchdown run to win the game that is guaranteed to become part of Falcons history. The "run" is a highlight reel of its own. Here's how it played out.

*I*n a span of 7.3 seconds, Michael Vick manages to star, direct, and produce an instant NFL classic during overtime at Minnesota on December 1, 2002.

Facing second-and-8 with 12:47 left in overtime, Vick has Darrin Chiaverini lined up wide left, Trevor Gaylor wide right and tight end Reggie Kelly on the line of scrimmage next to left tackle Bob Whitfield.

Vick drops back to pass and rolls left, going as far back as the Atlanta 45 when he sees Eric Kelly covering Chiaverini tightly near the left sideline and former Falcon Ronnie Bradford shading Reggie Kelly, who has run into the left flat.

"Coming out of the pocket, when I saw the guys down field, they had their backs turned, and I knew I had the opportunity to run it," Vick says.

When it's clear Vick is going for the end zone, linebacker Nick Rogers turns away from Whitfield and begins pursuit.

Vick crosses the 50 with Rogers and left end Lance Johnstone bearing down on his right. As he reaches the Minnesota 45, Rogers and Johnstone are behind him. Five other Vikings are giving chase on either side of Vick, but cornerback Corey Chavous and linebacker Greg Biekert have the best angles.

Chavous, who was deployed to protect against a long pass, has his back to the end zone but runs from the left side of the field to midfield. Biekert bears down to Vick's right.

WHEN WORLDS COLLIDE

As they converge at the 22, the laws of physics say Vick is going down. Instead, he turns on another jet to dart between Chavous and Biekert. The latter flattens the former as the Vikings turn Keystone Cops, and Vick is nearly in the clear.

"Coming out of the pocket, when I saw the guys down field, they had their backs turned, and I knew I had the opportunity to run it," Vick says.

Eric Kelly is behind Vick, and cornerback Brian Williams tries to take angle from the right, like Biekert. They're too late. Mr. Vick outruns them all. He receives no significant downfield block on arguably the greatest ad-lib play in franchise history.

"One of my greatest attributes is my vision," he says. "What I see looking

WHAT I SEE LOOKING DOWNFIELD, I SEE SO CLEARLY. I TAKE AN ANGLE AND I'M THINKING END ZONE ALL THE WAY. —MICHAEL VICK

down field, I see so clearly. I take an angle I know guys can't get me at. That's what I was trying to do out there. I'm just thinking end zone all the way."

RUN FOR THE TUNNEL
Vick keeps running, all the way into the tunnel that leads to the visiting team's locker room. Team publicists Aaron Salkin and Frank Kleha corral Vick and bring him back to the field for a TV interview. Vick is grinning from ear to ear as he unsnaps his chin strap and pushes the helmet up so his faceguard is pointing toward the Metrodome ceiling.

Among the first to greet him is one happy head coach. "Yep," Dan Reeves says with a big smile. "Just the way I drew it up."

Among the first to greet him on the sidelines is one happy head coach. "Yep," Dan Reeves says with a big smile. "Just the way I drew it up."

CHAPTER **EIGHT** 121

CHAPTER NINE
REALITY CHECK
2002 REGULAR SEASON—GAMES 13-16

12.08.2002 FALCONS vs. TAMPA BAY BUCCANEERS

PLAYING THE BUCS

They won the war today, but this is the second of many, hopefully, in my career. This will be my rivalry. —Michael Vick

TAMPA. The NFC South comes full circle. Atlanta wins two close games against New Orleans. The Saints earn two close victories against Tampa Bay. The Bucs drill the Falcons twice.

TOUGH BUCS DEFENSE
With super star linebacker Derrick Brooks leading the way, the Bucs defense, including the fab front four of Warren Sapp, Simeon Rice, Anthony McFarland, and Greg Spires, holds the Falcons to only 68 yards rushing—86.5 under an average that ranks No. 3 in the NFL. The Falcons convert only three of 12 third-down opportunities. Of the first seven possessions, five are punts, plus an interception, and a field goal.

DOWN DAY
Michael Vick's numbers hardly live up to the pregame hype of his being a top candidate for the league's Most Valuable Player award. A week after gaining 346 total net yards, Vick has just 140, including only 15 rushing.

QUOTES OF THE DAY:
"We didn't put a cape on his back," Simeon Rice says, "the rest of the world did. We just took it off. I don't think he anticipated what he got today."

Maybe so, but just maybe this game is the beginning of a good old-fashioned rivalry in the NFC South.

Against the eventual Super Bowl champions, Vick and Atlanta's offense struggle all afternoon. The Falcons have the football 12 times but manage drives of 20 yards or more just twice. Vick is sacked twice and knocked down several times.

122   ATLANTA FALCONS

Receiver Trevor Gaylor has the play of the day against the Buccaneers—a 47-yard pass reception—on the Falcons' only touchdown drive of the afternoon.

Played at Tampa Bay > > > Attendance: 65,648 > > >

INDIVIDUAL LEADERS: RUSHING > Atlanta: *Duckett 13-47* > Tampa Bay: *Alstott 13-95*
PASSING > Atlanta: *Vick 12-25-125 1 td, 1 int.* > Tampa Bay: *B Johnson 23-31-276 4 tds*
RECEIVING > Atlanta: *Crumpler 2-25 1 td* > Tampa Bay: *Jurevicius 8-100 2 tds*

FINAL SCORE:

Buccaneers **34** Falcons **10**

Atlanta	0	3	0	7	**10**
Tampa Bay	0	21	6	7	**34**

TEAM STATS 12.08.2002

	Atl	TB
First Downs	10	22
Total Net Yards	181	421
Rushes-Yards	23-62	29-150
Passing Yards	119	271
Passes Comp-Att-Int	12-25-1	23-31-0
Sacked-Yards	1-6	1-5
Penalties-Yards	4-45	5-38
Fumbles-Lost	0-0	0-0
Time of Possession	26:02	33:58

2nd Quarter
TB–Jurevicius 10 pass from Johnson (Gramatica kick)
TB–Jurevicius 13 pass from Johnson (Gramatica kick)
Atl–Feely 30 FG
TB–McCardell 14 pass from Johnson (Gramatica kick)

3rd Quarter
TB–Gramatica 42 FG
TB–Gramatica 21 FG

4th Quarter
Atl–Crumpler 5 pass from Vick (Feely kick)
TB–McCardell 27 pass from Johnson (Gramatica kick)

Patrick Kerney makes five tackles and a sack against Tampa Bay, but the Buccaneers still manage 421 yards on offense.

CHAPTER **NINE**

12.15.2002 FALCONS vs. *SEATTLE SEAHAWKS*

PLAYING THE SEAHAWK

Those guys came out there, and they wanted it more than us. That's what it comes down to. They blitzed us well. They caught us off guard a little bit. —Warrick Dunn

ATLANTA. No one feels worse than Jay Feely. The second-year kicker pushes a 36-yard field goal attempt that would've given Atlanta its second overtime victory in the past 15 days and helped secure a playoff spot. Instead, Seattle, needing seven plays to drive 74 yards, wins on Shaun Alexander's 27-yard run.

Feely takes the blame for the miss, adding that snapper Derek Rackley and holder Chris Mohr made no mistakes. "It was perfect. I just missed it," Feely says, his face downcast and his words minced. "I let my team down."

WEST COAST BLUES

Yes, a good kick might have erased some bad memories from the previous week, but the defense isn't exactly up to speed. The Falcons just can't solve a West Coast offense that, if it's on, can fatigue the strongest defense.

"We allowed them to make some third downs and keep drives alive where we just completely turned guys loose,"

Linebacker Sam Rogers (93) and the Falcons have their hands full against quarterback Matt Hasselbeck and the Seahawks. "We stopped them twice on fourth down and forced three turnovers," says defensive coordinator Wade Phillips, "but it wasn't enough."

Played at Atlanta > > > Attendance: 69,551 > > >

INDIVIDUAL LEADERS : RUSHING > Atlanta: *Dunn 20-101* > Seattle: *Alexander 28-127 2 tds*
PASSING > Atlanta: *Vick 38-21-240 2 tds, 2 int.* > Seattle: *Hasselbeck 31-22-298 1 td*
RECEIVING > Atlanta: *Crumpler 5-75 1 td* > Seattle: *Robinson 9-143*

Michael Vick's fourth-quarter drive helps make up for two interceptions and a fumble but Atlanta's offense struggles in the second half against Seattle, scoring on only one of six possessions.

coach Dan Reeves says. "Whether it's communication with the safeties, with the corners, getting in the right thing, we've got to get that resolved because you just can't do it."

SOMETIMES IT'S JUST NOT ENOUGH
"We stopped them twice on fourth down and we had three turnovers, and it just wasn't enough," new defensive coordinator Wade Phillips says. "In overtime, I think everybody thought we were going to make the field goal and we didn't. I think we let down a little bit. I've got to get with them and say, 'Hey, we've got to get ready. It could happen.' "

VICK RHYMES WITH PICK
Though Michael Vick produces another last-second touchdown to force overtime as he completes a 12-yard bullet to Trevor Gaylor on fourth-and-eight, the offense isn't without fault.
Cornerback Willie Williams gives the Seahawks a 21-17 lead with a fumble

Continued on page 128

FINAL SCORE: (OT)

Seahawks 30 — **Falcons 24**

Atlanta	14	3	0	7	0	**24**
Seattle	7	0	14	3	6	**30**

Allen Rossum gives Atlanta a lift with a 91-yard kickoff return.

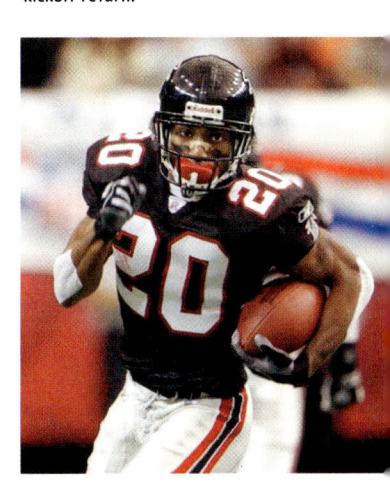

1st Quarter
Sea–Alexander 3 run (Lindell kick)
Atl–Rossum 91 kickoff return (Feely kick)
Atl–Crumpler 20 pass from Vick (Feely kick)

2nd Quarter
Atl–Feely 22 FG

3rd Quarter
Sea–Stevens 5 pass from Hasselbeck (Lindell kick)
Sea–Williams 25 fumble return (Lindell kick)

4th Quarter
Sea–Lindell 43 FG
Atl–Gaylor 12 pass from Vick (Feely kick)

Overtime
Sea–Alexander 27 run

TEAM STATS 12.15.2002

	Sea	Atl
First Downs	25	21
Total Net Yards	464	373
Rushes-Yards	37-166	35-150
Passing Yards	298	223
Passes Comp-Att-Int	22-31-0	21-38-2
Sacked-Yards	2-0	2-17
Penalties-Yards	7-45	11-95
Fumbles-Lost	4-3	1-1
Time of Possession	31:49	38:47

CHAPTER **NINE** 125

THE FANS

What kind of medicine does it take to build a healthy fan base for the Falcons? Arthur Blank and Dick Sullivan think all you need is a dose of common sense.

Arthur Blank assured the NFL that he understood the issues facing the fan base in Atlanta and wouldn't need long to make the appropriate corrections. In fact, Blank, Sullivan, and Reeves see the fans as the "12th man" on the field during every game. Their excitement and goodwill are vital to a winning franchise.

"We have good fans in Atlanta," Blank says. "They just need to be given an atmosphere they enjoy and the kind of customer service they truly deserve."

Blank, who personally answers fan e-mail, and Dick Sullivan conduct focus groups with fans to find out their likes and dislikes.

YA'LL COME—FALCONS WELCOME THE FANS

Slashing prices on thousands of season tickets generates immense goodwill. Season ticket sales in the upper-level end zones rise from 38 in 2001 to more than 10,000 by September. Tim Anderson, a fan from Alpharetta, is among those who respond instantly. His family had Bears season tickets when he was growing up and he wasn't about to pass up a chance to buy two season tickets at $100 a pop. "I didn't believe it at first," Anderson says from his upper-deck seat. "But I figured I couldn't go wrong for that price."

Giving fans a chance to tailgate in parking lots around the Dome helps create excitement too. Says Dick Sullivan, "Many fans said part of the whole experience with football is tailgating. Now we're able to provide tailgating." Improved traffic flow, increased police presence, and better quality and selection of food also add to the total football experience.

For eager kids or other fans who arrive early, a grassy area named "Falcons Landing" between the Georgia Dome and nearby Philips Arena gives families a chance to play interactive games, listen to live music, and get their faces painted before the game.

Inside the Dome professional acts entertain the crowd at halftime and after the game. There are no commercials on the huge video screens during television timeouts.

"Putting a winning product on the field is number one, but it's not just that," Sullivan says. "It's more than a three-hour football game, just like the Kentucky Derby is more than a two-minute race. You go for the whole experience."

Though such moves might seem to be nothing more than common sense, rewards await those who make them happen.

SERIOUS COMPETITION

There's some serious competition for Georgia sports fans. College teams provoke intense loyalty. There's also professional baseball, hockey, women's soccer, and basketball. But the Falcons are making inroads and Georgians are beginning to adjust their radar.

Fans are taking a bargain-rate flyer on season tickets to see if the Falcons are for real. Blank's pledge to fill the Dome with happy customers is starting to come true.

You may not see a tuxedo or a ballgown in the Georgia Dome during a Falcons game, but you will see some expressive dressing up. Young or old, it's fun to put on a little face paint or a funky wig and whoop it up.

Abb Hayes of Gainsville says, "I figured I'd at least check it out and go to some games and see what the atmosphere was like. The seats were way up there in the end zone, but I felt like I got my money's worth."

Hayes and Anderson are proof that the "the 12th man" theory works. They are local fans looking for a great game day experience and are willing to support the team. Providing what the fans want is the easiest way to combat visiting teams turning the Dome into an "away home game."

LISTEN AND LEARN

Blank says, "We just listened to the fans, gave them what they wanted, and took away the barriers that were there before."

THANKING THE FANS—PERSONALLY

On September 9, 2002, the entire Falcons team including Michael Vick, Warrick Dunn, T.J. Duckett, Bob Whitfield, and Keith Brooking showed up unannounced at various metro Atlanta locations to say thank you to the fans for being "the 12th man." Outfitted in full uniform, they made stops at "secret" locations—such as Lenox Mall, CNN Center, The Varsity, Gwinnett County Fire Department, a North Dekalb Quik Trip, and the Kroger Citi Center in East Point—thrilling unsuspecting fans by presenting them with autographed thank you cards, lapel pins, and even some good old-fashioned hugs.

CHAPTER **NINE**   127

Warrick Dunn's third 100-yard effort isn't enough to save the Falcons at home in the Georgia Dome against Seattle.

Continued from page 125

return late in the third quarter. Blitzing through the right side of the Atlanta line, Williams knocks running back Warrick Dunn into Vick, who fumbles at midfield. Williams stops only long enough to pick up the ball and run in for the score.

Seattle contains Vick most of the afternoon and picks him twice. Cornerback Ken Lucas has both interceptions, the first of which ends the Falcons first drive and sets up Alexander's 3-yard touchdown run.

"Those things are going to happen," Vick says. "That's only my sixth interception of the year. That's not many for a first-year starter. I don't get discouraged."

QUOTE OF THE DAY

Patrick Kerney doesn't want to see heads hanging and bottom lips sticking out at team headquarters in a couple of days. The defensive end traces the roots of this defeat to seeing some players "feel sorry for themselves" after the Tampa Bay loss.

"Hopefully there's going to be one hell of a sense of urgency around the facility this week to know that we're playing for a whole hell of a lot," Kerney says. "Things are going to be upbeat at the facility this week. I can promise you that. Guys are going to be flying around at practice."

Seattle's first drive of the second half ends when Heath Evans fumbles and Patrick Kerney recovers the ball.

CHAPTER **NINE**

GAME 15

12.22.2002 FALCONS vs. *DETROIT LIONS*

PLAYING THE LIONS

WINNING SOLVES A LOT OF PROBLEMS. IT MAKES PEOPLE FORGET ABOUT THE PAST AND LOOK TOWARDS THE FUTURE. —WARRICK DUNN

ATLANTA. The Falcons handle Detroit at home, then realize how close they are to the team's seventh playoff spot in 37 years. In the final week of the regular season, they'll be able to clinch a berth if …

The New York Giants lose to Philadelphia or the New Orleans Saints lose to Carolina, or the Giants (9-6) and Saints (9-6) both win and Atlanta (9-5-1) beats the Browns.

"The main thing is trying to get there," says Warrick Dunn, who made four postseason trips in five years at Tampa Bay. "Get in the playoffs and then whatever happens happens." To prove his point, he carries the ball a career-high 30 times and rushes for 132 yards and a crucial 3-yard touchdown in the fourth quarter.

QUENTIN-SSENTIAL
Michael Vick is effective as well,

Jay Feely hits five field goals as the Falcons score on eight of 13 possessions against Detroit and put together seven drives of 47 yards or longer. Meanwhile, the Lions offense is no match for Mark Simoneau and the Falcons defense.

TEAM STATS 12.22.2002

	Det	Atl
First Downs	12	27
Total Net Yards	208	533
Rushes-Yards	21-87	41-197
Passing Yards	121	336
Passes Comp-Att-Int	11-33-3	20-38-1
Sacked-Yards	3-28	1-1
Penalties-Yards	9-86	7-55
Fumbles-Lost	0-0	1-1
Time of Possession	21:42	38:18

Played at Atlanta > > Attendance: 69,307 > > >

INDIVIDUAL LEADERS: RUSHING > Atlanta: *Dunn 30-132 1 td* > Detroit: *Stewart 12-34*
PASSING > Atlanta: *Vick 20-38-337 2 tds, 1 int.* > Detroit: *McMahon 11-33-149 2 tds, 3 ints.*
RECEIVING > Atlanta: *McCord 7-182 1 td* > Detroit: *Schroeder 2-60*

FINAL SCORE:

Falcons **36** — Lions **15**

Atlanta	3	10	6	17	**36**
Detroit	0	0	0	15	**15**

1st Quarter
Atl–Feely 23 FG
2nd Quarter
Atl–Feely 23 FG
Atl–McCord 20 pass from Vick (Feely kick)
3rd Quarter
Atl–Feely 36 FG
Atl–Feely 20 FG
4th Quarter
Atl–Feely 39 FG
Det–Stewart 1 pass from McMahon (McMahon-Schroeder pass)
Det–Cason 15 pass from McMahon (Hanson kick)
Atl–Dunn 3 run (Feely kick)
Atl–Finneran 34 pass from Vick (Feely kick)

completing 20 of 38 passes for a career-best 337 yards and two touchdowns. His primary target is second-year receiver Quentin McCord, a seventh-round draft pick from Kentucky who was signed off the practice squad in October.

Of McCord's seven catches, six go for first downs and another for a 20-yard touchdown that gives the Falcons a 13-0 lead with 17 seconds left before halftime.

McCord's final reception is on the first drive of the third quarter. He beats safety Brian Walker on a deep route for a 60-yard pass to the Detroit 7.

"That's the type of receiver I am," McCord says. "I'm aggressive. I like to attack the defense. Every time I touch the ball I'm thinking touchdown."

FEELY'S BACK
Jay Feely adds his fifth field goal early in the fourth

Warrick Dunn gets another 100-yard game, and this time it helps Atlanta to victory.

CHAPTER **NINE**   131

132 **ATLANTA** FALCONS

quarter for a 22-0 lead. "That's what I tried to focus on this week," he says, "just being fundamentally sound." Feely sets a franchise single-season record with 128 points, besting Morten Andersen's 122 in 1995.

NOT SO FAST
The Falcons allow the Lions to play catch-up in the fourth quarter—for a while. Detroit comes to within seven points but Michael Vick, Warrick Dunn, Brian Finneran, and the offensive line fight back.

"We certainly had some adversity in the fourth quarter," Dan Reeves says. "The Lions got within seven points, so we really got through some tough times and we matured a little bit." Dunn saves some of his best for last. He pounds the Lions with 51 yards rushing in the fourth quarter on 10 carries.

QUOTE OF THE DAY
"Winning solves a lot of problems," Dunn says. "It makes people forget about the past and look toward the future."

It's a big day for Falcons past and present: Quentin McCord makes seven catches; legendary linebacker Jessie "The Hammer" Tuggle who retired in 2001, is honored at halftime in the Georgia Dome; Keith Brooking makes six tackles; and Brian Finneran gets the Falcons final touchdown on a 34-yard pass from Michael Vick.

CHAPTER **NINE**

12.29.2002   FALCONS vs. CLEVELAND BROWNS

PLAYING THE BROWNS

ANY DOORWAY TO THE PLAYOFFS IS A GOOD ONE—EVEN IF IT'S THE BACK ONE. THE FALCONS SNEAK INTO THE POSTSEASON EVEN AFTER LOSING TO THE BROWNS. THEY JUST DON'T KNOW WHO THEY'RE PLAYING.

CLEVELAND. The only good news this week is Carolina's victory at New Orleans, which guarantees Atlanta the sixth and final NFC playoff spot. But the Falcons fly home unsure of their opponent and postseason destination.

BLANK GIVES REEVES THE NEWS

On Atlanta's final drive, the team learns of New Orleans' loss to Carolina when an announcement is made over the PA system. Arthur Blank approaches Dan Reeves, who's facing the field, holding his clipboard and wearing a headset. Before he calls the next play, Reeves pulls back his headset and listens as the first-year owner congratulates him on making the playoffs.

"If anything, it was a shock because I didn't think Carolina would win," Reeves says. "The last time I saw the score was real early and New Orleans was ahead, 3-0. I never really thought about it after that."

When Michael Vick airs it out—he attempts 40 passes in the regular-season finale against Cleveland—Falcons receivers are on the move. Tight end Alge Crumpler hauls in two passes for 34 yards against the Browns.

134   ATLANTA FALCONS

ed at Cleveland > > > Attendance: 73,528 > > >

INDIVIDUAL LEADERS: RUSHING > Atlanta: *Dunn 20-67* > Cleveland: *Green 27-178 2 tds*
PASSING > Atlanta: *Vick 17-40-240 1 td, 1 int.* > Cleveland: *Holcomb 7-14-86 1 td, 2 ints.*
RECEIVING > Atlanta: *Finneran 3-77 1 td* > Cleveland: *Johnson 3-32 1 td*

JUST GET THE CHANCE TO PLAY

Even if the Falcons aren't happy with the loss, they're still in the playoffs. Frustration brings some questions about playcalling, but Bob Whitfield has a more stoic approach.

"Everybody has his druthers about what they would like to run. If you ask me, I would like to run the tackle-eligible and have me go on a corner route and catch the ball and be celebrating with a touchdown. But that ain't going to happen, so whatever they call, the O-line blocks. Period. That's how it works."

Brian Finneran is another receiver with a big game, making three catches for 77 yards against Cleveland.

QUOTE OF THE DAY

Whitfield also appreciates the eight field goals Jay Feely has kicked in the past two games, but the 11-year veteran still wants more touchdowns.

"If we played soccer, we'd be World Cup champs," Whitfield says. "But we ain't playing soccer."

FINAL SCORE:

Browns **24** — Falcons **16**

Atlanta	0	7	9	0	**16**
Cleveland	3	7	0	14	**24**

1st Quarter
Cle–Dawson 40 FG

2nd Quarter
Cle–Green 21 run (Dawson kick)
Atl–Finneran 15 pass from Vick (Feely kick)

3rd Quarter
Atl–Feely 42 FG
Atl–Feely 49 FG
Atl–Feely 30 FG

4th Quarter
Cle–Johnson 15 pass from Holcomb (Dawson kick)
Cle–Green 64 run (Dawson kick)

TEAM STATS 12.29.2002

	Atl	Cle
First Downs	16	17
Total Net Yards	331	318
Rushes-Yards	27-105	34-189
Passing Yards	226	129
Passes Comp-Att-Int	17-40-1	14-25-3
Sacked-Yards	2-14	3-25
Penalties-Yards	4-27	4-25
Fumbles-Lost	4-2	1-1
Time of Possession	29:15	30:45

Linebacker Matt Stewart makes eight tackles, including this sack of Kelly Holcomb.

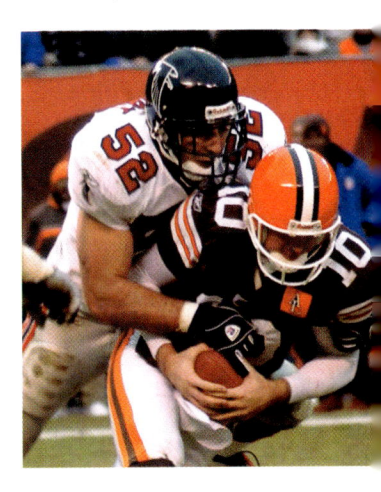

CHAPTER **NINE** 135

CHAPTER TEN
MAKING BELIEVERS—
THE

2002 PLAYOFFS— GREEN BAY AND PHILADELPHIA

*I*t might be freezing in Green Bay, and maybe the Falcons don't see a lot of snow down in Georgia, but, in this exciting year, they'd go to the moon to be in the playoffs.

"It's amazing what you can accomplish when everybody tells you something can't be accomplished. The thing is that we never stopped believing in ourselves, even when everyone said we backed into the playoffs last week," Atlanta free safety Keion Carpenter says after intercepting Brett Favre twice in a stunning 27-7 wild card upset.

PLAYOFFS

When the Falcons hit Lambeau Field, it's chilly on the sidelines... but the team's stunning victory in the NFC wild card game warms the hearts of fans throughout Georgia. It was the Packers' first home playoff loss in history.

CHAPTER TEN

1.04.2003　　FALCONS at *GREEN BAY PACKERS*　**WILD CARD GAME #1**

PLAYING THE PACK

WILD CARD

WINNING AT LAMBEAU FIELD IS A FULL TEAM EFFORT AS ATLANTA TAKES THE PACKERS TO TASK IN COLD AND SNOWY GREEN BAY.

GREEN BAY. The Falcons are supposed to be frozen solid by the time they hit Lambeau Field. Instead, they defy the odds as no visiting team has done in the long and illustrious history of the Green Bay Packers. As they prepare to kick off to the Falcons, the Packers are 11-0 at Lambeau, 13-0 overall in home playoff games.

NUMBERS THAT NUMB

Green Bay quarterback Brett Favre, a lock to one day become the 20th Packer inducted into the Hall of Fame, is 15-0 at Lambeau when the temperature on the field is 34 degrees or less. The Falcons, who have zero players or coaches in the Hall of Fame, enter with a 12-25 record on prime time TV. Green Bay hasn't had a losing record in 10 years. The Falcons have never had consecutive winning seasons. And yet, Atlanta becomes the first team to win at Green Bay since the 2001 Falcons, who left town with a 23-20 victory.

Continued on page 144

The snow at Green Bay's Lambeau Field doesn't bother either the Falcons offense or Patrick Kerney (97) and the defense.

138　**ATLANTA** FALCONS

Played at Green Bay > > > Attendance: 65,358 > > >

INDIVIDUAL LEADERS: RUSHING > Atlanta: *Dunn 15-64* > Green Bay: *Green 11-34*
PASSING > Atlanta: *Vick 13-25-117 1 td* > Green Bay: *Favre 20-42-247 1 td, 2 int.*
RECEIVING > Atlanta: *Dunn 4-40* > Green Bay: *Walker 5-104*

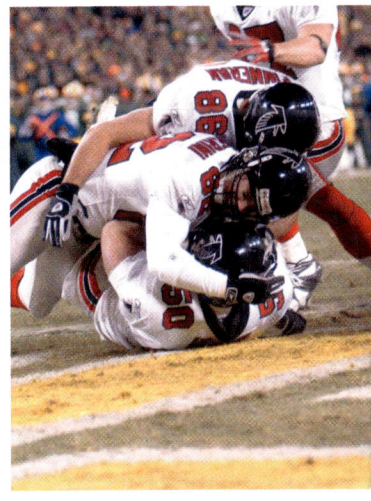

FINAL SCORE:

Falcons **27** — *Packers* **7**

Atlanta	14	10	3	0	**27**
Green Bay	0	0	7	0	**7**

The Falcons force five turnovers from a Green Bay team that ended the regular season with an NFL-high 45 take-aways and tied Tampa Bay for the league's best turnover margin at plus-17.

1st Quarter
Atl–Jefferson 10 pass from Vick (Feely kick)
Atl–Ulmer 1 return of blocked punt (Feely kick)

2nd Quarter
Atl–Duckett 6 run (Feely kick)
Atl–Feely 22 FG

3rd Quarter
GB–Driver 14 pass from Favre (Longwell kick)
Atl–Feely 23 FG

TEAM STATS 1.04.2003

	Atl	GB
First Downs	21	17
Total Net Yards	309	289
Rushes-Yards	44-192	19-56
Passing Yards	117	233
Passes Comp-Att-Int	13-25-0	20-42-2
Sacked-Yards	0-0	2-14
Penalties-Yards	3-20	3-15
Fumbles-Lost	1-0	3-3
Time of Possession	36:04	23:56

CHAPTER **TEN** 139

When Atlanta picked T.J. Duckett 18th overall in the 1st round, he thought it was a joke. Why would a

T.J. DUCKETT

team with Anderson and Dunn want another back? It all becomes clear in the playoffs.

T.J. **DUCKETT** Running Back

A first-round pick, Duckett proved he was a durable and talented rusher at Michigan State, where he had 3,379 career yards and was a second-team All-American as a junior.

Having decided to skip his senior year at Michigan State, T.J. Duckett waits out the 2002 draft, expecting Cleveland to select him with the 16th pick. But the Browns choose Boston College running back William Green, and Duckett settles in for a longer wait. He's barely paying attention when the Falcons take him in the 18th overall spot. Duckett is stunned. Atlanta? Warrick Dunn? Jamal Anderson? Maurice Smith?

CHAPTER **TEN**   141

I DO EVERYTHING FOR MY MOTHER. SHE'S THE REASON I'M HERE, THE REASON I GET UP EVERY DAY AND GIVE THANKS FOR THE BLESSINGS GOD HAS GIVEN ME. —T.J. DUCKETT, WHOSE MOTHER DIED OF CANCER IN MARCH 2001.

At 6 feet and 254 pounds, T.J. Duckett shows the power to run over NFL defensive backs and the speed to run past opposing defensive linemen. In his rookie season, he finishes second on the team to Warrick Dunn in rushing attempts and is Atlanta's third-leading rusher.

"I completely thought it was a joke," Duckett says. "My heart started beating, and it was a big blur. All I heard was 'Atlanta' and 'Falcons' and me saying, 'Sure.' That's all I remember."

RHYME AND REASON
The Falcons do, however, have a plan. On June 1, Anderson is released, and Duckett spends the next month in passing camp learning the offense. After a nine-day holdout in late July, he finally takes the practice field.

"It was my first practice, so I was nervous, but I was excited to get out there," Duckett says.

REDEMPTION
Duckett's rookie season has its ups and downs, a combination of injuries and some ineffectiveness. Finally, in the wild card win at Green Bay, Duckett returns as a force, running 17 times for 43 yards. His 6-yard touchdown proves Duckett can impact the Falcons problems in short-yardage situations.

His rookie season is a roller-coaster ride, but Duckett never loses focus. Off the field he's starting a foundation to help women stricken with cancer. The disease killed his mother, Jacquelyn Barham, in March 2001.

"I just want to be able to help anybody else who's going through that same thing," Duckett says. "Whatever I can do to help, I'm all for it."

2002 INDIVIDUAL STATS / T.J. Duckett

Rushes	130
Rushing yards	507
Receptions	9
Receiving yards	61
Touchdowns	4

#45

CHAPTER TEN 143

Continued from page 138
STOKED
Packers coach Mike Sherman watches in frustration as Michael Vick and Shawn Jefferson connect on a 10-yard touchdown pass on the opening drive. Then Green Bay kicker Ryan Longwell hooks a 47-yard field-goal attempt.

It's about to get worse. The Green Bay offense, which controls the ball for all but 58 seconds of the final 7:27 of the first quarter, is ready to start the second period, but the Packers muff a punt return, and George Layne recovers for the Falcons.

Mark Simoneau and Artie Ulmer give the Falcons a 14-0 lead midway through the first quarter. Simoneau blocks Josh Bidwell's punt from the end zone, and Ulmer recovers the loose ball for his first career touchdown. T.J. Duckett's 6-yard run gives the Falcons a 21-0 lead.

Atlanta maintains possession for the final 6:34 of the second quarter.

Duckett runs for 13 yards and Warrick

While T.J. Duckett and the Falcons run out the clock on the field in their NFC wild card victory, owner Arthur Blank congratulates his team on the sidelines in Green Bay.

144 ATLANTA FALCONS

His first NFL playoff game is against the Packers and quarterback Brett Favre, but Michael Vick still comes up a winner. Vick rushes 10 times for 64 yards, in addition to passing for 117 yards and scoring one touchdown.

Dunn for 21 before Vick produces another jaw-dropping play. Packers defensive end Kabeer Gbaja-Biamila appears to have Vick trapped along the Green Bay sideline. But Vick pushes the 255-pound Gbaja-Biamila away and turns around to run toward midfield on a 12-yard gain. "I'm speechless," the Green Bay defender says. "He's elusive."

STUFFED

Ellis Johnson makes the biggest defensive play of the game. With 6:37 remaining in the second quarter and Atlanta leading 21-0, the Packers stand fourth-and-goal at the 2 when Johnson corrals running back Ahman Green for a 4-yard loss.

Green, who abused the Falcons for 155 yards in the season opener, finishes with 34 yards on 11 carries before a bruised knee forces him to leave in the third quarter. His problems reduce the options available to Favre, whose 54.4 passer rating is his second-lowest of the season.

Favre and Donald Driver account for Green Bay's lone score, a 14-yard TD pass in the third quarter, and the Falcons are on their way to Philly.

Patrick Kerney celebrates the victory before the Falcons think about their next playoff game—at Philadelphia.

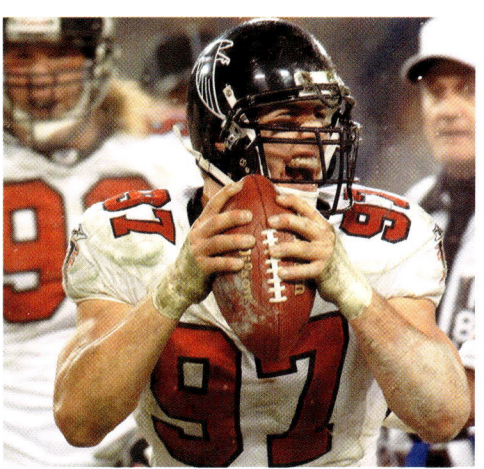

CHAPTER TEN 145

ON THE ROAD AGAIN
TRAVELING WITH THE TEAM

TAKING CARE OF THE FALCONS —PLAYERS, COACHING STAFF, AND A FEW SCOUTS—IS NO SMALL CHORE. BUT BRIAN BOIGNER AND HIS TEAM RUN THE EQUIPMENT ROOM LIKE A SMALL STORE. "I GUESS YOU COULD SAY WE RUN A MINIATURE HOME DEPOT," SAYS BRIAN BOIGNER WITH A SMILE.

Brian Boigner is a detail man. As the Falcons equipment manager, he ensures that every player has what he needs seven days a week from the end of March through the end of the season—hopefully very late in January.

The busiest time of year is before training camp as Boigner and his three-person staff prepare to pack four semi-trailer trucks full of equipment for the 120-mile drive to Furman University in Greenville, S.C. At Furman, the Falcons will need about 120 helmets; 130 shoulder pads; 450 T-shirts; several hundred knee; thigh and hip pads; approximately 800 socks; and about 300 pairs of shoes. And everything has to be waiting when they arrive. Don't forget extra cleats. And tape, lots of it. Screwdrivers, hammers, pliers, staple guns, scissors—definitely need those. Coolers, thousands of paper cups. Four practice jerseys—two white and two black—for each player.

"I guess you could say we run a miniature Home Depot," Boigner says.

KEEPING BUSY

When 2003 camp begins July 23, Boigner is ready to accommodate 86 players, 18 coaches, a few scouts, and other football operations employees who cycle through.

"I've come up with a little itinerary; I go over it and fine-tune it every off-season," Boigner says. "We check it off as we pack it, whether it's 35 additional helmets or 40 additional shoulder pads. Usually we bring four practice jerseys for each player and what we call 'dead numbers' to give to players we sign during training camp, which we always do."

During the regular season, he's dealing only with 58 players—53 active and 5 on the practice squad, but the pace hardly slows.

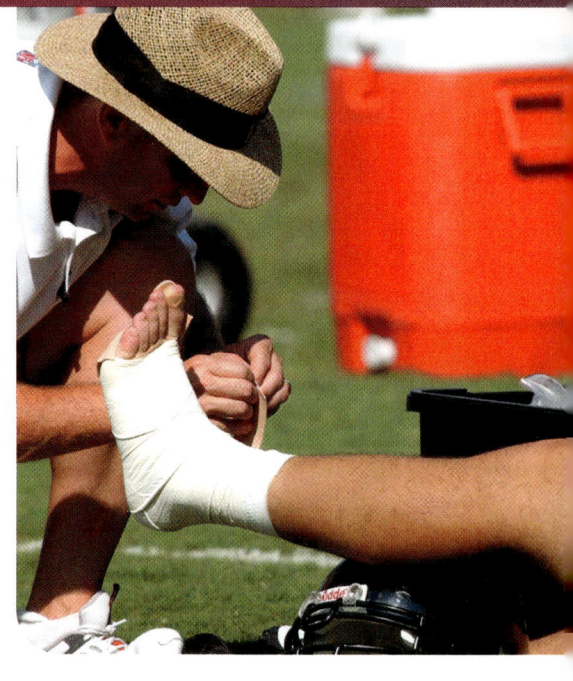

How many rolls of tape? How many ankles? With 86 players in camp in July, the Falcons training staff has to show plenty of stick-to-itiveness.

Boigner and his staff—senior equipment assistant Horace Daniel, a team employee since 1968; assistant equipment manager Jimmy Hay; and assistant equipment manager Jason Baisden—are fortunate that the Falcons break training camp three days before the first preseason game.

"Obviously, every game is a road

ATLANTA FALCONS

game since we have to go down to the Georgia Dome," Boigner says of the 45-mile drive to Atlanta. "We pack up a 40-foot truck and hit the road."

Actual road games require more logistics. Saturday mornings a truck heads straight to Hartsfield International, where the team charter is waiting. Boigner checks in about an hour after the truck leaves Flowery Branch to make sure it arrives. In the destination city, another truck hauls the gear to the stadium.

Also instrumental in moving the team are logistics manager Spencer Treadwell and facilities manager Cecil Mullins who are responsible for everything from team transportation to hotel rooms.

TOTAL CARE

The Falcons equipment staff takes care of everything for the players.

"The only thing we ask them to pack is a special brace or cast," Boigner says. "Other than that, we don't leave too much up to them. Recently signed Linebacker Keith Newman told me about a linebacker in Buffalo who forgot his helmet—twice. You talk to some of the (equipment) people with other teams who might say the players have got to do their part, but the way I see it—that's our job." Stadiums with poor field conditions need extra shoes and cleats. "If you're playing a game on a surface that's had some questions in the past, I make sure they have the shoes they need for that surface," Boigner says.

CHECKING OFF

"My staff and I go through each bag and make sure there's a helmet in there, shoulder pads in there, hip pads, thigh pads, knee pads, and there are the correct shoes in there. We take care of that stuff Monday through Friday and then Saturday and Sunday is pretty smooth."

Special players require special treatment. Boigner always packs four helmets for Michael Vick. He did the same for Jamal Anderson, which paid off in 2000 when Anderson's helmet was stolen before a game in San Francisco.

"For Michael, I bring three extra helmets," Boigner says. "I keep one on my trunk on the field with me and I have two others in reserve.

"I take extra precaution with Mike's stuff. Things people might be tempted to take won't even be in a bag marked 'Vick.' "

CHAPTER **TEN** 147

1.13.2003   FALCONS vs. PHILADELPHIA EAGLES   **NFC DIVISIONAL GAME**

PLAYING THE EAGLES

IT'S BEEN A GOOD YEAR. —COREY SIMON

*P*HILADELPHIA. So many times on this frigid night the capacity crowd at Veterans Stadium tries to rattle Michael Vick and his teammates.

Finally, with 4:14 remaining, the Falcons succumb. Vick hangs his head at midfield after completing a 5-yard pass to Brian Finneran that falls 5 yards short of a first down and effectively ends Atlanta's Super Bowl dreams.

The phenomenal Atlanta quarterback smiles, though, as Hugh Douglas, the Eagles star defensive end, meets him facemask-to-facemask and offers congratulations for fighting so hard. Turning to walk to the sidelines, Vick also hears a compliment from defensive tackle Corey Simon. "It's been a good year," the lineman says.

CHILLY RECEPTION

It comes as no surprise that Philadelphia is the stronger team on a night when the wind-chill dips to 15 degrees. The Eagles enter as the NFC's top seed, and their 38 victories over the past three years are the most in the NFL.

"It was a tough game, and they kept coming after us, much more than I expected," Vick says. "We just kept trying to make things happen, but we couldn't get over the hump."

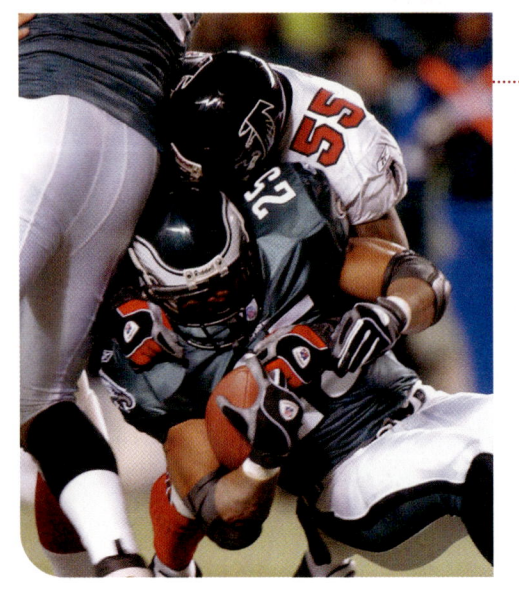

Despite their rough start, the Falcons hang tough. Neither team scores in the third quarter and Atlanta enters the fourth only a touchdown behind. In the end the Eagles hang tougher and the Falcons 2002 season comes to an end in Philadelphia.

TEAM STATS   1.13.2003

	Atl	Phi
First Downs	19	15
Total Net Yards	354	318
Rushes-Yards	24-93	26-91
Passing Yards	261	227
Passes Comp-Att-Int	23-39-2	20-30-0
Sacked-Yards	3-27	2-20
Penalties-Yards	9-95	3-30
Fumbles-Lost	2-0	2-0
Time of Possession	30:33	29:27

148   ATLANTA FALCONS

Played at Philadelphia > > > Attendance: 66,452 > > >

INDIVIDUAL LEADERS: RUSHING > Atlanta: *Dunn 14-45* > Philadelphia: *Staley 18-63*
PASSING > Atlanta: *Vick 38-22-274 2 int.* > Philadelphia: *McNabb 30-20-247 1 td*
RECEIVING > Atlanta: *Finneran 5-76* > Philadelphia: *Thrash 2-77 1 td*

FINAL SCORE:

Eagles **20** — Falcons **6**

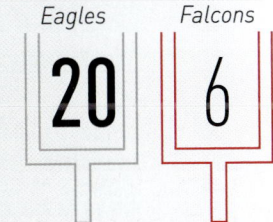

Atlanta	0	6	0	0	**6**
Philadelphia	10	3	0	7	**20**

1st Quarter
Phi–Taylor 39 int. return (Akers kick)
Phi–Akers 34 FG
2nd Quarter
Phi–Akers 39 FG
Atl–Feely 34 FG
Atl–Feely 52 FG
4th Quarter
Phi–Thrash 35 pass from McNabb (Akers kick)

THE BIG PLAY

With 6:34 remaining and the Eagles leading 13-6, Donovan McNabb faces fourth-and-1 when he completes a 35-yard touchdown pass over the middle to James Thrash.

So much is made of McNabb's two-month layoff from a broken ankle, but the super star quarterback hardly looks rusty. After the TD strike, which ends the Eagles six-quarter drought without an offensive touchdown, McNabb has completed 20 of 30 passes for 247 yards and no interceptions.

The season may be over, but the future has begun.

QUOTE OF THE DAY

"It's frustrating, but I never felt like we didn't keep trying to make plays," Warrick Dunn says. "I've never played in a game where penalties (95 yards) seemed to be deciding the outcome of a game that early. That just put us so far back."

CHAPTER **TEN**

150   ATLANTA FALCONS

CHAPTER 11

THE START OF A NEW ERA— CRAFTING A WINNER

In Arthur Blank's first 12 months as owner the Falcons sign four players to highly lucrative contracts. Linebacker Keith Brooking and defensive end Patrick Kerney agree to deals that keep them in Atlanta and some exciting new talent arrives at the complex in Flowery Branch.

Less than a year after running back Warrick Dunn leaves Tampa Bay to become Blank's first major acquisition, receiver Peerless Price comes on board.

The recruitment of Price sets a new Falcons standard for doing business. Buffalo can prevent Price from leaving. As a restricted free agent, he is "tagged" as a "franchise player," meaning the Bills can retain him in 2003 with a one-year, $5.01 million contract—the average of the NFL's five highest deals for receivers based on 2002 salary cap dollars.

Peerless Price and his daughter, left, take to the microphones at the press conference announcing that they're about to become part of the Falcons family. Above, Price and Arthur Blank display his new jersey. Price says that the atmosphere Arthur Blank is creating around the team made the decision to come to Atlanta an easy one.

CHAPTER **ELEVEN** 151

THE PRICE IS RIGHT

Price can land a much bigger deal in the open market, and the Bills, who lack a first-round pick in the '03 draft, give him permission to pursue a trade. Price lives in Lithonia, about 20 miles east of downtown Atlanta. He instructs his agent, Tim McGee, to be aggressive in reaching a deal with the Falcons.

By March 7, Price is standing next to Blank at a news conference in Flowery Branch. Sixteen days have passed since Buffalo "tagged" Price, but plenty of maneuvering takes place before the Falcons obtain a top-flight receiver to pair with quarterback Michael Vick.

Ron Hill, Atlanta's vice president of football operations, works the phones with Buffalo general manager Tom Donahoe, who insists on obtaining the Falcons' first-round pick, No. 23 overall, in 2003. Hill offers either a second-round pick or a first-round spot in '04, but Donahoe says no.

Meanwhile, Ray Anderson, Atlanta's chief administrative officer, negotiates the parameters of a long-term contract with McGee. The two sides are still seven days away from reaching an agreement as Blank applies a full-court press.

Price is visiting his mother in their hometown of Dayton, Ohio when the NFL's free agency period begins February 28. The Falcons call Price and want to know if he can drive to Cincinnati and board Blank's private jet for a flight to Atlanta.

"By the time I landed, my mom was calling me to tell me she had received some roses from Mr. Blank," Price says. "Then me, my fiancé, and my agent sat down at his office in Buckhead. He wanted to hear what my vision was. He listened to what I had to say.

"He told me, 'Whatever you want, we can do' as far as my family, setting up a foundation and getting settled into a new home."

Peerless Price speaks to reporters at the March 7, 2003 press conference annoucning that he's become a Falcon. Great things are expected of this former Bills star.

SERVICE WITH A SMILE

Next comes a tour of the Georgia Dome, where the Falcons use a recruiting ploy that's a common staple for major universities. Price, who played at Tennessee and helped the Volunteers win a national championship in his senior year of 1999, had seen this before.

"We walked into the Georgia Dome, all the lights were out and it was like going to a college because when I walked in, it said, 'Welcome, Peerless Price,'" Price says. "That's when they put the tape on the Jumbtron."

Pulling out all the stops, Dick Sullivan produces a Price highlights video including edited segments of Peerless on the receiving end of some Michael Vick passes. A recording of "Welcome to Atlanta," the summer hit single by hip-hop sensations Jermaine Dupri and Ludacris, jams from the loudspeakers as Price watches his future partnership in action. "It was unbelievable," Price says. "Me catching balls, but it made it seem like Mike Vick was throwing them."

The next day, Price will take an obligatory tour of the Falcons' complex, but he is far more impressed with Blank's hospitality.

"We went to Arthur's home for dinner that night," Price says. "You don't get that many owners invite you to dinner. It was real cool, made me feel real comfortable, like somebody I could approach. Some owners, you're scared to approach—or at least talk to and have a real conversation with. That's the way he made me feel, my family feel, my agent feel. It was second to none, the way I was treated."

He tells McGee to cancel trips they plan to take to Washington and San Diego.

"It all worked the way it was supposed to, I guess," Price says. "David Boston goes to San Diego, Laveranues Coles to Washington, me here."

CORY HALL GETS SOME CHOICES

Defensive coordinator Wade Phillips tells former Cincinnati safety Cory Hall he can choose between playing free safety or strong safety. Price knows he will be the No. 1 receiver. Former Green Bay cornerback Tyrone Williams understands when he signs that he'll be replacing cornerback Ashley Ambrose on the right side of the secondary.

On March 3, Hall has just visited the Houston Texans when he arrives in Atlanta.

"I met all these wonderful coaches, and I met the owner, Mr. Blank," Hall says. "I was telling him last night that

Defensive coordinator Wade Phillips told former Cincinnati safety Cory Hall, below, that he could choose between playing free safety or strong safety. " I was just impressed, and it was apparent they want me here." says Hall who cancelled trips to see two other teams." There was no need," Hall says. "This is a family-type atmosphere, and I like that."

Keith Newman, former Buffalo linebacker, left, and Tyrone Williams, cornerback from Green Bay, right, were both impressed with the reception they received in Atlanta. Keith Brooking, right, signed a new deal because he wanted to stay. Word is spreading around the league that the Falcons are becoming a destination team.

he may have said more words to me last night than any words I heard from the owner in my four-year career in Cincinnati. I was just impressed, and it was apparent they want me here. I was blown away last night by Mr. Blank."

Hall cancels trips to two other teams.

"There was no need," Hall says. "This is a family-type atmosphere, and I like that. I'll do anything for my family, and I feel that here. Everyone—from coaches and owners, to everyone else—was like a family. It was different here. I didn't get that sense even in Houston. Once I got here, I didn't even entertain the thought of going anywhere else."

THE MARTAY JENKINS STORY

Blank has grown accustomed to hearing new players tell him they're canceling other visits. The Falcons land former Arizona receiver MarTay Jenkins in a similar, but scaled-down, fashion.

The team buys Jenkins a first-class seat, and he flies into Hartsfield International Airport, where a limousine is waiting for him. Though his visit to the complex only takes a couple of hours, Jenkins is told that his hotel room and rental car will be covered.

Players all have a nose for business, and there's no doubt that money is the biggest factor in negotiations. Finding a home on and off the field is important too. Real estate agents have already been contacted and are only waiting for him to call. Blank, Anderson, Hill, Sullivan, and Coach Reeves are all attending the NFL spring meetings in Phoenix while Jenkins visits, but they all pass a phone around the table during dinner and tell him how pleased they are that he wants to become a Falcon.

"When I came here, I had a few other visits lined up, a few other teams I could've chosen from," Jenkins says. "But the whole vibe that I got here, the atmosphere, what they're doing—they were so excited—then talking to the offensive coordinator about how the offense is run—I was definitely looking past the one-year deal.

"They set me up with different apartments, gave me directions to restaurants and shopping centers, those kind of things."

Jenkins calls his agent and tells him to discontinue talks with Oakland, Jacksonville, and Houston.

ELLIS JOHNSON COMES ON BOARD

Defensive lineman Ellis Johnson lands in the Falcons' lap in August 2002. Having asked for and received his release from Indianapolis after failing to buy into the new defense being installed by new Colts coach Tony Dungy, Johnson is coveted by several teams who need a seven-year starter to plug a hole.

"After watching the techniques that they're teaching on film, it was like these are things that I've done before," Johnson says. "I'd be really comfortable doing it. I knew I'd need not go anywhere else."

KEITH BROOKING STAYS AT HOME

Blank loves baseball and considers himself a big Braves fan. He remembers some of the feelings Tom Glavine expressed after signing a contract to play for the New York Mets.

Glavine said his old team didn't make the kind overtures he received from the Mets and Philadelphia Phillies. Blank looks at Brooking's impending free agency and wants to make sure the Falcons don't take Keith for granted.

On the Monday before teams have to apply franchise or transition tags, Brooking and his girlfriend have dinner with Blank and his wife at the owner's home. The "tag" deadline passes, and the Falcons declare they either will sign Brooking or let him wade into unrestricted free agency.

"My personal experience as an agent was that the franchise tag benefited nobody unless the player or the team was being totally unreasonable," Anderson says. "We decided two weeks ago we weren't going to tag Keith. I've seen too many cases, even if a lengthy contract is worked out, where you don't have the same player you had before."

A week later, Brooking signs a new, seven-year contract. Frustrated that negotiations had stalled too long, Brooking personally calls Blank to express his desire to sign before unrestricted free agency begins February 28.

Brooking doesn't want to move from metro Atlanta, where he's lived his entire life. "I realize other guys are going to sign after me that aren't as good as me, or maybe on that same level, that are probably going to blow on past me," Brooking says. "But I said I want to be here so I'll take less.

"Hey, don't get me wrong. This is great money, unbelievable money, really. OK, say I could've gotten more on the open market. Fine. But one thing you can't put a price on is peace of mind. What's the price of being able to play in the NFL and have your family so close? To me, that's worth a lot. Playing for the Falcons and working for Mr. Blank just makes it that much better."

Keith Brooking had options as a free agent—a number of teams would have been happy to have him. In the end staying near home and family made his decision to stay in Atlanta the right one for all concerned.

THE EXTRA MILE

Players around the league are beginning to notice that something special is happening on the field in the Georgia Dome and at the team headquarters in Flowery Branch. The Falcons are working hard to sign the best players the NFL has to offer and to keep them happy once they've joined the team.

On the last Friday night in February 1998, the Falcons learned some disappointing news. Atlanta was negotiating with Ty Detmer, an unrestricted free agent and former starting quarterback for the Eagles, to back up starter Chris Chandler. Detmer turned down the team's offer—a multiyear contract with an average salary of $1.3 million—for a lesser deal with the cash-strapped San Francisco 49ers.

Not long thereafter, the Falcons were foiled in an attempt to sign Eric Zeier, a restricted free agent with Baltimore, when the Ravens retained his services by matching Atlanta's offer. Next they turned to former Washington QB Mark Rypien, a backup in St. Louis in 1997, but his son's illness prevented him from playing.

Thus did the Falcons enter their Super Bowl season with 44-year-old Steve DeBerg as the No. 2 quarterback. DeBerg hadn't taken a snap in the NFL since 1993.

BREAKING TIES—RECRUITING IN THE NEW ERA

If an equivalent scenario begins to unfold with Arthur Blank as owner, director of pro personnel Les Snead likes Atlanta's chance of signing its first choice.

"We always had the resources before Arthur bought the team to do what was necessary to recruit a player," says Snead, who begins his sixth year with the team in 2003. "The difference now is that we're able to break a lot of ties."

Snead lists several other factors that help steer free agents toward the Falcons:

- One of Blank's first moves was to build a players' lounge at team headquarters. He let the players design and furnish their hangout and equip it with the latest gadgets.
- As a reward for each victory Blank began a Friday custom of specially catered luncheons consisting of lobster, steak, shrimp, and barbecue. The new owner serves the food himself and front-office executives wait on the players and coaches.
- The facilities, thanks to the Smith family's decision to move to Flowery Branch in 2000, are all new.

"When someone is hungry you give them something to eat." Arthur Blank and the front office team now serve catered luncheons to the team on the Friday following each victory.

The team took Blank up on his offer to let them design and equip the players' lounge at the Falcons complex in Flowery Branch.

- Quarterback Michael Vick will be only 23 when the 2003 season opens giving the team some solid room to mature.
- Season-ticket sales are expected to top an all-time high of 62,000. NFL spokesman Greg Aiello says the Falcons set a league record for existing franchises by registering a 100-percent increase from 2001 to 2002.

THE WORD IS OUT

"Players talk among themselves, and word gets out pretty quickly about which teams might have the best atmosphere to work in and those that might not," Snead says.

"It's pretty clear based on feedback we've gotten from hundreds of people that the Falcons have something special going on."

FANTASTIC

LOOKING TO THE FUTURE

I PERSONALLY WILL NOT REST UNTIL I HAVE AN OPPORTUNITY TO WEAR A SUPER BOWL RING ON BEHALF OF EVERYBODY IN ATLANTA AND EVERYBODY IN THE STATE OF GEORGIA. THAT'S AN IMPORTANT GOAL OF MINE, AND I'LL TELL YOU THAT I'M NOT GOING TO REST UNTIL THAT TAKES PLACE. —ARTHUR BLANK

On April 24, 2003 the Falcons introduced a snappy new look for the team. Freshly designed uniforms are another reflection of Blank's commitment to moving the team into a new era.